USES OF TRADITION IN RUSSIAN &
SOVIET ARCHITECTURE

VICTOR AND ALEXANDER VESNIN, COMPETITION PROJECT FOR THE HEAVY INDUSTRY COMMISSARIAT, RED SQUARE, MOSCOW, 1934

Front Cover: Ivan Leonidov, project for a Victory Monument on Red Square, 1957 (courtesy Andrei Leonidov, Moscow); *Inside front cover*: 17th-century church of Voskresenia v Kadashakh, Moscow, watercolour by St Petersburg architect P P Fetisov, from 5th *Annual of the Society of Artist-Architects*, St Petersburg, 1910

TEMPLE AT GARNI, ARMENIA, 4TH CENTURY

△D Architectural Design Profile 68

USES OF TRADITION IN RUSSIAN &
SOVIET ARCHITECTURE

G GOLTS, PROJECT, 1944 (COURTESY N GOLTS)

IA CHERNIKHOV, SECTORAL VOLUMES, c 1930

ST BASIL'S CATHEDRAL, MOSCOW, 1555-61

Editor: Dr Andreas C Papadakis

First published in Great Britain in 1987 by *Architectural Design*
an imprint of the
ACADEMY GROUP LTD, 7 HOLLAND STREET, LONDON W8 4NA

Architectural Design Profile 68 is published as part of *Architectural Design* Volume 57 7/8-1987
Distributed in the United States of America by
St Martin's Press, 175 Fifth Avenue, New York 10010

ISBN: 0-85670-920-4 (UK)

Translations by Catherine Cooke and Lyudmila Burke

Printed in Great Britain by E G Bond Ltd, London

EDITORIAL

Catherine Cooke

EARLY 19TH-CENTURY HOUSE, N A OSTROVSKY STREET, MOSCOW

This issue of *AD* originated in an invitation made by Andreas Papadakis and myself to Anatolii Poliansky, President of the Soviet Union of Architects, at the time of the UIA Congress in Cairo. I recall a very cold Moscow morning where Oleg Shvidkovsky and myself discused it in greater detail with the President in his office at what in the West would be called a 'breakfast meeting'. It ran to twice the scheduled length as they elaborated my proposed theme for the issue, and the same enthusiasm has attended the whole venture. A related exhibition is coming to Britain at the same time.

I proposed this theme as one central to Soviet architectural, indeed aesthetic, philosophy. 'The uses of tradition' coincides as nearly as possible to that central principle of the Socialist Realist method known as 'critical assimilation of the heritage'. With refreshing lack of jargon they refer to it here as 'tradition and modernity' – *traditsiia i sovremennost'* – a phrase embodying the aspiration they have pursued since the 1930s of finding some synthesis between what remains culturally valid from the past and what is best in the new – be that technical or social – to produce a work which remains accessible to its public. If these notions have a familiar ring in the West too these days, that is precisely why I proposed this topic.

The pictures above and opposite encapsulate the point which recent history has taught us all, East and West: that 'the heritage' and cultural continuity reside as much – even perhaps more – in the general character of the environmental fabric as in individual monuments of great architecture. Contributions from all over the Soviet Union in this issue make this point repeatedly. The Soviet press is now as full of public and professional protest about the irreplaceable cultural losses perpetrated by ruthless 'modernisation' as our own. Bureaucratic rigidity and battles between different economic power groups are no respectors of the ideological divide in this field. As Shvidkovsky writes here, it is 'the new young talents' whose contribution 'will be indispensible' in future. Their imaginative and constructive focus on the human experience of space, and the possibilities for its aninmation in the public domain, have become a very positive feature of the Soviet architectural scene.

Some of the individual articles here result from direct invitations by myself. I am particularly grateful to Elena Borisova and Evgenia Kirichenko for the historical perspective they have provided, which is intended to show something of the attitudes and experience that the Soviet profession inherited from the 19th century alongside specific buildings. Some names in Andrei Bokov's 'exhibition' will already be familiar through their successes in *AD*'s Dolls Houses and House for Today competitions, as well as other international contests. In thanking Professor Ilya Lezhava from the Moscow Architectural Institute for his work on the thematic section of this issue with fellow lecturer Andrei Nekrasov and with Vyachislav Glazychev, I should record his role over many years as stimulus to the young, in encouraging them to stretch their imaginations and design abilities through these conceptual competitions. As they frequently complain, we have far too few of them.

On *AD*'s behalf I should like to record our great appreciation to all the four organisations which have made time and material available to produce both this issue and the exhibition: the Union of Architects itself, the Moscow Architectural Institute, the Union of Soviet Friendship Societies and the Shchusev State Research Museum of Architecture. None of the logistics would have been possible without the help of Galina Kolobova of *Dom Druzhby* in Moscow, and I thank her most sincerely.

Dedications are not normal in this location: happily they are not often appropriate. But I am sure my Soviet colleagues will not demur if I dedicate this issue to the memory of Alexei Gutnov, a member of the planning team for it who died so tragically young during its preparation. Few people contribute to architecture on so many fronts with such consistently penetrating relevance and originality. In the 1960s he was one of the so-called NER group which I can best identify as a 'Soviet Archigram'. In the Moscow Strategic Planning Bureau he was a pioneer of mathematical modelling techniques; I translated some of his work elsewhere in the late 1970s. In every forum and on every issue he was in the best sense provocative. Deeply steeped in what Russians call 'architectural culture' (a concept as lacking as its substance in so many Western circles), he was a brilliant and charismatic teacher, to whom many projects in urban revitalisation already owe their genesis. The article published posthumously here is typical, and a not inappropriate memorial.

INTRODUCTION

Anatolii Poliansky

Peace and housing – these are the problems which the 20th century has made the most urgent of our era. The very first decree of the Soviet government after it took power in the 1917 Revolution was that 'On Peace', and only a few weeks later it began the process of resettling the Russian workers into more adequate housing. This was the order in which the Soviet state saw its responsibilities, and the right to housing became enshrined in the Soviet Constitution.

The task of the architect is conceived in those terms: as the provision of facilities for public and personal activities, of community buildings and, first and foremost, of housing. Through the 70-year existence of the Soviet Union the task has been solved with varying levels of quantitative and qualitative success, as the changing technical and economic conditions have permitted. Had it not been for the Second World War leaving 25 million Soviet citizens homeless, we should undoubtedly have solved the housing problem by now. As it is, we stand at something of a turning point after Government and Party have launched a new integrated programme dedicated to providing every family with its own individual apartment or house of modern standard by the year 2000.

In professional terms, the present state of affairs on this front is far from simple, and it is the focus of many debates concerning the larger field of architectural activity at present, which my colleagues discuss elsewhere in these pages. The key problems relate to the development of the building industry's industrial base, and the methods of design incorporated in standardised projects, which are the two foundations of mass housing construction in our country. It is precisely these which for the last three decades have generated, and continue to generate, an historically unprecedented speed and volume of new construction. But the time has come when the level of refinement of industrial processes and the state of standardised planning are lagging behind the sharply rising aesthetic and spiritual requirements of the society we are building for.

It is in response to this problem that numerous distinctively regional schools have grown up within our multi-national profession in recent years, each of them basing its approach on its particular understanding of its traditions. If one phrase could describe the present state of Soviet architecture, it would be 'unity in diversity'. A universal social standard is realised in different ways according to the great differences in climatic conditions and ethnic character in different republics, and in the resulting historical traditions of culture.

This interest in tradition and the vernacular, in the nation's history and culture, is manifested very visibly amongst architects concerned with the treatment of the historic environments found in old town centres. Literally within one generation, attitudes to this question have totally changed. Thus today one may talk of towns growing in two different directions: outwards, through new construction, and inwards, through restoration and reinstatement of the apparently outlived historic fabric. My colleagues demonstrate in some examples that this process is still not very well established. Its approaches and skills of design as well as of technical restoration still have to be developed. Even the last-mentioned requires a sophisticated combination of great erudition and great ability, and a strong feeling for contemporaneity which seems at first sight paradoxical. Both the moral responsibilities and the aesthetic problems involved in this restoration work depend on a genuinely in-depth understanding of the eras which produced the buildings concerned.

The restorers who recreated Leningrad's great palace complexes from nothing after the vandalism perpetrated on them during the Second World War acquired worldwide fame. Not for nothing is that war known to us as the Great Patriotic War. Today however matters of restoration and reconstruction, whether of individual buildings or relatively large areas of urban fabric, are only one part of a larger policy for planning and urban design which aims both to preserve what exists, and to create vigorous towns of distinctive individuality for the future. The transformation of Minsk is a fine example – perhaps our best at present – of the quality of result which is possible with city-scale action when the objectives are clearly formulated and realistic, and the town's future is in the hands of intelligent, talented people.

This is the situation we aspire to achieve nationwide, but each region, republic, city, throws up its own problems and its own ways of resolving them. I hope that the publication of this special issue of *Architectural Design* will make it possible for more people to get some idea of what our problems are today, how Soviet architects are solving them, and of how they see things developing in the future.

Talking of new trends in our architecture, I would like to end by underlining the most fundamental and important one. Architects are now remembering that architecture is an art; an art with vast educative and nurturing potential, whose duty it is to reflect the spiritual values of its age and to produce some degree of harmony between need and environment both for society as a whole, and for each individual within it.

Professor Anatolii Poliansky is President of the Union of Architects of the USSR

TRADITION AND MODERNITY
Whither Soviet architecture today?

Oleg Shvidkovsky

It is hard for individuals born in an age still perfumed by the 19th century, before television, and when horses were still more common than motorcars on our streets, to adapt to the speed at which the third millenium is approaching. My generation entered its youth during the battle with fascism. Time stood still on the whole, and we were motivated by a desire to resist rather than create change, to keep our balance, as we were swept along by the pressures of a struggle to the death. I recall how in 1945 we returned to the architectural institute in our army greatcoats, and it was a long time before we shed the field shirts and boots whch had been through the war with us. 40 years ago, time moved more slowly than today.

Hardly a day passes now which does not bring some new material or more efficient technique to building. If you go away somewhere for a few months you risk finding your street unrecognisable on your return. The city is changing its shape with impetuous haste and inevitability. The stylistic features and images of architecture may change more slowly, but here too my generation has seen at least three sharp changes of direction already, and right now a fourth is becoming discernable. It may be that the aesthetics of architecture are changing even faster in the West: I think this is so. In the socialist countries movement is slow, like an armada of heavy sea-going ships, and very rarely is there a complete change of tack. But in the West the constant shifts could be described by a sailor as 'yawing about'. Suddenly a mass of diverse directions are being pursued simultaneously, a multitude of 'microstyles' develop; novelty and originality are chasing rapidly changing tastes and creating them as they go.

Whether the actual architecture changes with it or not, rapid changes in the living environment as a whole have created breaks in the thread connecting us to the past. That dishonourable pseudo-innovative injunction to 'sweep all the dust of history from our towns' has been used to justify the mindless throwing out of those aesthetic traditions which have permeated our culture over time. Tradition represents for me the most advanced experience of a people and their professional architects at a particular moment. What one age considered to be of long-term value leaves its mark permanently on the consciousness of succeeding generations. Tradition is as diverse as it is complex. The manner in which it affects our own lives is often surprising; it may illuminate our work unnoticed, but the process of assimilation is always difficult, hindered by incomprehension or simply the primitive character of our city building culture.

Pure engineers can provide perfectly adequate 'roofs over heads', but I find myself increasingly seeking something on a higher, more spiritual plane, an independent culture of city-building which closely reflects the *Weltanschauung*, without levelling out the differences between peoples and cultures in aesthetic matters. We discuss acute social problems and throw aesthetic ones into the background, as if the most important social issues could be solved in isolation from society's moral and spiritual advancement, which is embodied in the process of creating aesthetic images and codes.

It is precisely to the spiritual plane, to humanity's conception of the beautiful, that architectural traditions most directly relate, whether through its own form, or that of nature, or in the harmony between the two. Expressive architecture, just like nature, nourishes the emotional life of man. The grey and faceless, on the other hand, stifles emotion and deadens feeling, destroying the innate aesthetic sensibilities and taste cultivated in a nation through the cumulative experience of generations. And it is these dead senses which will determine the 'laws of beauty' on which the next generation will build.

From very ancient times there has existed a Russian tradition whereby 'a building place' was chosen 'in relation to the whole world'. This notion of 'a place congenial to building' (*stroinoe mesto*) is essentially untranslatable, combining both functional and value-laden concepts. This was how locations for churches and other honoured buildings were chosen, creating nodal points in a network of man-made structures in the countryside, or the major ensembles of a town. Most commonly these sites were the high places, given an emphasis by nature which the architecture placed on them would reinforce.

Another strong tradition in Russia was to develop the profile of a building, particularly a stepped, layered manner. Polychromy and 'transparency' were two other important elements of traditional building, which proceeded on the moral principle that one did not obstruct a neighbour's view of the overall beauty of the urban panorama.

The peoples of the Central Asian republics have their own equally ancient traditions of course, making up a culture of city building which is quite different. One might mention the tradition of building on a 'carpet' pattern; of closed 'family' spaces in the traditional houses; of special irrigational systems which left their mark on the whole fabric of a settlement. And the astonishing decorativeness of their architecture, embracing complex traditions of ornamental inscriptions; the clear colours of sky-blue cupolas harmonising so perfectly with the soil and the mud-built structures. Wherever one looks, in the republics of the Baltic or the Transcaucasus, in the expanses of the Ukraine or Belorussia – everywhere in the Soviet Union we encounter the

7

OLEG SHVIDKOVSKY

impact of very distinctive local tradition.

In the 1960s all this was thrown out as having no significance in an age of industrialised housing construction. Out went the variety of colour and form which had provided so simply and effectively national architectural traditions in our towns and villages. In came standardised plans, housing blocks identical to each other like peas in glass preserving jars.

Perhaps this was itself a sign of the times. Perhaps it is to be expected that innovation, the rejection of tradition and new aesthetic preferences should emerge as the characteristics of an age of industrial and social renewal. But why should the architecture of socialist countries enjoy some special right to spiritual sterility? Nowhere can architecture be turned into an industrial product off a conveyor belt: convenient, comfortable, but culturally barren and far removed from genuine art. Beauty no less than utility shapes the spirit of an individual, and in architecture no less than in painting or sculpture, music or poetry.

We foolishly regard as outdated the old saying that 'architecture is the mother of the arts'. Architecture may not always be the natural mother, but she certainly remains the step-mother to all genuine artistic creativity. It is the urgent task of architects today, as I see it, to reinstate the direct parental relationship once more.

I hear the habitual and far from harmless objection: 'Don't you understand that the most important thing today is to give every family its own independent home – to solve the cursed housing question (as Engels called it) for the first time in history.' To my generation, living all its childhood and youth in overcrowded apartments shared by several families with a communal kitchen, this lofty aim is more than close to our hearts. I have the deepest respect for our country's aspiration to a solution of this problem at its roots. But it is also clear to me that amidst the complexity of today's problems we get nowhere by relegating the moral, ethical and aesthetic aspects of the housing problem to second place. We have a saying that 'the road of

Tomorrow usually leads to the city of Never'. We are beginning to grasp the truth of this at last.

It is the designers themselves working on each particular job, and not the theoreticians, who must sort out the specific means of aesthetic revitalisation: but deep-rooted cultural traditions are their essential helpmate in attaining that goal.

One thing is clear today: we have to find some kind of equilibrium between technology and art whereby both can develop simultaneously. Here, it seems to me, lies the area for genuine innovation in architecture today. We know from history that the development of real architectural innovation, that is the development of architecture as an art, has not always proceeded in direct synchrony with the development of technology. There have repeatedly been periods when several quite different aesthetic systems have been erected upon the same building technology. This is equally possible today. But architecture probably achieves the greatest depth and verity when technological and constructional discoveries are integrated with aesthetic ones; when technological development receives some of its impetus from the challenges of aesthetics.

The language of architecture has to be enriched, developed, and with it the formal and emotional complexity of its spatial structures. This will not be achieved by the pursuit of either tradition or innovation at the expense of the other, but only by bringing the two together in a general upgrading of ability within the architectural profession. Indispensible will be the contribution of new young talents, capable of making those aesthetic discoveries which will sustain our work not just for a year or two, but for centuries. That should be the lifespan of a genuine classic work of architecture.

Professor Oleg Shvidkovsky is Director of the Sector for Soviet Art and Architecture of the Institute of Art History, Moscow, and President of the Soviet National Committee for ICOMOS

A HISTORICAL SURVEY IN COLOUR

Traditional architectures and their reworking

from the medieval period to today

All Photographs except Melikhovo by Catherine Cooke

TIMBER *IZBAS*, ZVENIGOROD NEAR MOSCOW, 19TH CENTURY

Photo Igor Palmin

LANDSCAPE AND ORIGINS: CHURCH NEAR CHEKHOV'S COUNTRY COTTAGE AT MELIKHOVO, NEAR MOSCOW

EARLIEST CLASSICAL INFLUENCES   ASSUMPTION CATHEDRAL, KREMLIN, MOSCOW, 1475-9, *(LEFT);* ARCHANGEL CATHEDRAL, KREMLIN, BY ALOVISIO NOVO, 1510-8, *(RIGHT)*

MOSCOW BAROQUE, CHURCH OF INTERCESSION AT FILI, 1690-3

V BAZHENOV, PALACE AT TSARITSYNO, MID 18TH CENTURY

CATHEDRAL ON TSARS' ESTATE AT KOLOMENSKOE, EARLY 17TH CENTURY

KAZAKOV & ZHILIARDI, MOSCOW UNIVERSITY, MID 19TH CENTURY

TYPICAL 'URBAN ESTATE', MOSCOW: THE MAIN HOUSE

'URBAN ESTATE': SIDE WING OF COURTYARD

O BOVE, CHURCH OF ALL MOURNERS, MOSCOW, 1830s

O BOVE, CATHEDRAL OF DANILOV MONASTERY, RECONSTRUCTION 1985-6

TON'S BYZANTIANISM: KREMLIN ARMOURY, MID 19TH CENTURY

V SHERVUD, HISTORICAL MUSEUM, 1875-82

A VASNETSOV, 'OLD MOSCOW', 1904, OWNED BY F SHEKHTEL

F SHEKHTEL, DEROZHINSKAIA'S MANSION, MOSCOW, 1902

V VASNETSOV, TRETIAKOV GALLERY 1902: DETAIL

BRICK DOME OF TEMPLE VESTIBULE, SAMARKAND

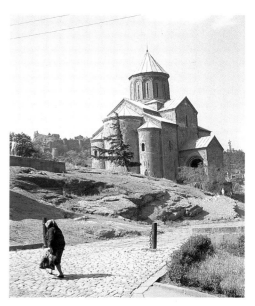

MEDIEVAL CHURCH, TBILISI, GEORGIA

SOUTHERN TRADITIONS

13TH-CENTURY TILES IN AFROSIAT, DRAWN BY PETERSBURG ARCHITECT N N K-SHCHERBIN (*OAKh ANNUAL*, 1910)

TEMPLE DOORWAY, SAMARKAND

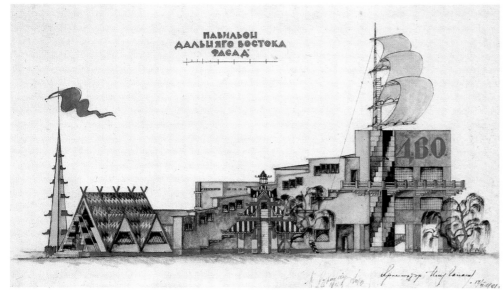

I GOLOSSOV, 'FAR EAST' PAVILION, AGRICULTURAL EXHIBITION, MOSCOW 1923

SAMARKAND: THE OLD CITY

13

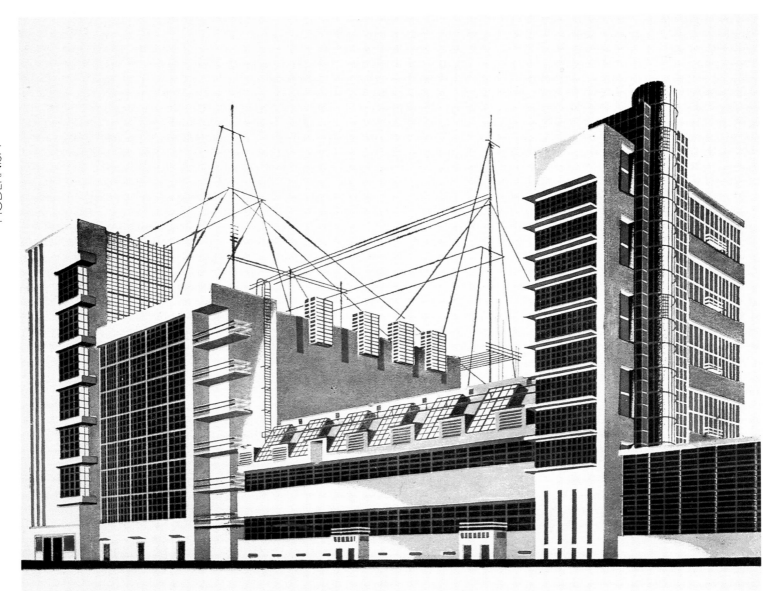

IAKOV CHERNIKHOV, ARCHITECTURAL FANTASY NO 30: 'STRICT CONSTRUCTIVE FORMS IN QUIET COLOURS', c 1929

MOISEI GINZBURG, HOUSING 'OF TRANSITIONAL TYPE', ROSTOKINO, MOSCOW, 1939-31

K MELNIKOV, OWN HOUSE, MOSCOW, 1927-9

IVAN ZHOLTOVSKY, APARTMENT HOUSE ON MOKHOVAIA STREET, MOSCOW, EARLY 1930s

ZHOLTOVSKY, STANDARDISED URBAN CINEMA, MOSCOW, 1957

ZHOLTOVSKY, SUBURBAN APARTMENT BLOCK, MOSCOW, 1957

M POSOKHIN ET AL, MODEL HOUSING DEVELOPMENT AT NORTH CHERTANOVO, MOSCOW, UNDER CONSTRUCTION 1977

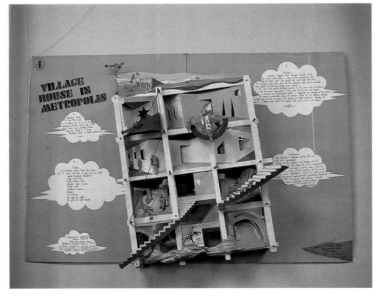

PUSCHUKEVICH, VELICHKIN ET AL, UNESCO SELF-BUILD HOUSING COMPETITION 1983

THEATRICALISED URBAN SPACE; STUDENT PROJECT UNDER I LEZHAVA

BREAKING WITH CLASSICISM
Historicism in nineteenth-century Russia

Elena Borisova

ELENA BORISOVA

VASILY POLENOV & VICTOR VASNETSOV, CHURCH AT ABRAMTSEVO, 1881-2

Until recently, that style of Russian architecture described by the term 'eclecticism' (one which basically corresponds to the concept of historicism) was considered to represent a period of artistic decline. It seemed impossible to explain how after the great artistic achievements of Russian classicism, a whole number of architectural masterpieces linked to Russia's triumph in the Patriotic War of 1812, could come a period where the aesthetic achievements of classicism were rejected. However, this was a process which was affecting the whole of Europe in the same way, while the individuality of the Russian solutions derived from the particularly complicated historical and political situation then obtaining.

In contrast to most European countries, where the transition from classicism to romanticism was smoother and more gradual, late classicism maintained a stronghold in Russia for longer, partly because it was widely seen during the 1830s, after the Decembrist uprising of 1825, as a visual expression of the most autocratic aspects of Tsarist rule. For this reason, the spread of romantic ideas and ideals has been invested by the most progressive thinkers in Russian cultural affairs with not only artistic but also important social significance. The liberation of creative work from the conservative canons of late classicism has been interpreted as representing a move away from academicism and the reactionary tendencies of officialdom.

The pursuit of the new tendencies in architecture and town planning, and rejection of the strict rules of classicism, was justified by the romantics as a manifestation of the artist's freedom of choice amongst art forms.

It should be said that the place of architecture in the structure of Russian artistic culture during the romantic epoch has only recently been subjected to attempts at precise definition, and even now remains the topic of extensive debate. Aside from its links with romantic aesthetics the source of the artistic conven-

tion of the three classical unities: place, time and action. As a result, an unprecedentedly lively historical awareness emerged, together with a historical method of thinking which thrived throughout the 19th century, leaving its mark not only on the academic outlook, but also on the artistic consciousness of the epoch.

The influence of historicism on Russian architecture in the second half of the 19th century can be traced in tendencies which on one hand were similar to those in Western European architecture, but on the other consciously reacted against them, (though the polemical disputes between Westernisers and Slavophiles about the two possible directions of future developments in Russia were not typical in architectural circles). For example, the inclination of romanticism towards the cultivation of its own national heritage was common both to Western Europe – where it first appeared as an interest in the Middle Ages and an enthusiasm for Gothic revival – and to Russia, where Old-Russian, pre-Petrine and folk architecture exercised a strong influence. But on the other hand, the search for a specifically national style of modern architecture in the second half of the 19th century produced results which sometimes owed

FROM LEFT TO RIGHT: MENELAS, TSAR'S 'COTTAGE', PETERHOF, 1826-9; A P BRIULLOV, CHURCH AT PARGOLOVO, 1831; N BENOIS, PALACE STABLES, PETERHOF

tions and inquiries which distinguished Russian architecture of the second half of the 19th century seem almost impossible to pinpoint. Romanticism not only shaped the newest tendencies in Russian artistic culture during the 1850s but went on to provide an impulse towards intense artistic exploration in many other fields during the rest of the century. During this process, romanticism itself altered in character, so that it became, in many aspects, the source for the national romanticism which emerged at the beginning of the 20th century.

The importance of specifically architectural developments in demonstrating the nature of artistic ideas in general during the romantic epoch in Russia cannot be underestimated. Architectural images provided the inspiration for poets, novelists, and artists, as well as absorbing the attention of architects themselves. The new architecture created the potential for a romanticised social environment, elaborated through a mesh of historical and literary associations. The 19th-century man felt himself to be direct heir to all that was most outstanding in the history of world architecture. Historical and stylistic eclecticism was an essential feature of this romanticism, so that it drew life from the expansion of international communications, and, with it, the conscious rejec-

less to Russian ideological sources than to European stylistic developments based on a return towards the sources of antiquity, the Renaissance and, primarily, the Gothic, which made the first breach in the seemingly immovable canons of classicism.

The Gothic, accepted as one of the most powerful expressions of the romantic outlook, entered the arsenal of artistic methods almost unnoticed and first revealed itself in Russia not in such literary forms as the tale of chivalry, or medieval ballad, but in architecture. On Russian soil the Gothic seemed to be a derivative, secondary phenomenon, which grew out of a whole complex of artistic views of romanticism, strongly influenced by romantic literature, and particularly English works. While the rebellious stance of Byron had a particularly strong appeal for the most convinced and progressively minded section of Russian artistic society, it was the work of writers such as Walter Scott which proved most important for the wider dispersal of these ideas. The influence of Scott's work was perhaps of less significance in literature than in Russian architecture of the 1820s to 1840s. The Gothic style took off as a perfect vehicle for the expression of romantic aesthetic concepts, despite the lack of native Gothic traditions, and was easily assimilated into the

ELENA BORISOVA

Russian artistic and figurative consciousness of the time. The first naive examples of Gothic architecture had appeared as early as the end of the 18th century, in the shape of works by Bazhenov and the architects of his circle. The sources of this local movement were to be found in aesthetic sentimentalism. Gothic first penetrated Russia via the English landscape garden, which, under the name 'natural' garden, became a widespread phenomenon. Interpretation of Gothic forms, which at the end of the 18th century were being taken from both Western European sources and Russian medieval equivalents, continued to take second place to the exploration of classical concepts, based on the aesthetics of the compact, balanced architectural volume and mass of the wall.

It was during the romantic epoch that the spatial achievements of Gothic were first noted. The principal novelty of the first Gothic buildings of 19th-century Russia lay in the treatment of the interior spaces. This marked the beginning of a new period in architecture when architects enjoyed using the decorative elements of Gothic for the opportunities they provided to exploit new constructional techniques and so create spaces freed from internal support and massive walls, as well as for the visual

las, is one of the earliest examples of the use of Gothic in domestic architecture. Churches and railway buildings were particularly well suited to the style. One of the first railway stations in Russia, at Pavlovsk, near Petersburg, was built by Shtakenshneider between 1836 and 1837 to Gothic designs. It seems that the reason for the choice of Gothic in this case lay not only in the desire to come closer to the English original, but also to generate associations with the real Gothic, which was the inspiration for the light airy space of the famous concert hall at the Pavlovsk Station.

The common feature of such buildings was not the form of architectural decoration itself, but rather the overall impression of unlocked, airy, infinite space.

In Western Europe the clearest embodiment of this tendency was Joseph Paxton's Crystal Palace, in London, where an ideal Gothic scheme with its longitudinal naves and transverse transepts was reduced to virtual immateriality. In Russia the same impression was achieved in less grandiose, but very diverse buildings.

The desire to achieve an accurate recreation of Gothic ideas was clearly demonstrated in the works of the architect Nikolai

ELENA BORISOVA

FROM LEFT TO RIGHT: SHTAKENSHNEIDER, LAKE PAVILION, PETERHOF, 1845-8; VON KLENZE, NEW HERMITAGE, ST PETERSBURG, 1839

link they provided with the Middle Ages.

The analysis of 19th-century architecture generally tends to concentrate on the historicism of its decorative features at the expense of its spatial characteristics. As a result, that peculiar 'historicism of space' which distinguishes Russian architecture of the second half of the 19th century, as much as any other, has been mistakenly neglected. Eclectic architects characteristically paid special attention to spatial solutions, and usually based them on precedents of a figurative rather than functional nature. One of the first Russian romantic architects, Alexander Briullov, stated that 'architecture is primarily the art of dividing and combining space'.

19th-century pragmatism was strangely permeated with romantic ideas, so that even the vast railway stations, the reading halls of large libraries, the covered markets, passages and exhibition pavilions which were the architectural achievements of the new century succeeded in expressing something of the apotheosis of the human spirit. These enormous enclosed spaces had much in common with the spatial structures of medieval architecture in the emotional response they stimulated in the user.

The 'Tsar's Cottage' in Peterhof (1828-29), by Adam Mene-

Benois, which were distinguished by their particular resemblance to their original models, along with the boldness and novelty of their spatial solutions. In an early work, the Court Stables complex in Peterhof (1847-54), the perspective of pointed arches and towers and the huge space of the riding hall were evidently inspired by medieval precursors. In the later Peterhof station (1854-57), the architect combined a double-arched Gothic portal surmounted by a tower with the metal structure of a covered platform, lit by huge pointed windows. Gothic reminiscences were interwoven here with innovative spatial solutions, creating a certain romantic fusion, which defines the character of the architectural image. This particular source of historicism was inspired not only by medieval architecture, but also by the heritage of classical antiquity, rather than Russian classicism. Architectural developments in this epoch owed much to the model provided by the Roman villa, which implemented a free, dynamic solution to the problems of volume and space. The picturesque, asymmetrical approach to volumetric composition, which in many ways anticipated 20th-century principles of free functional planning, was initially developed in Russian architecture by Gerald Bosse and Andrei Shtakenshneider.

In the palace at Mikhailovka near Peterhof (1857-62), Bosse created a dynamic composition. The palace is disposed along the diagonal axis of the site, made up, in the manner of a honeycomb, of separate cells which form a complex multi-surface spatial solution. The same method was used by Shtakenshneider in his series of park buildings in Peterhof, for instance in the 'Little Lakes', or 'Pink' pavilion which imitates the architecture of the Pompeian villas so popular with architects of this period. Antiquity takes on a more prosaic, down-to-earth character in their hands; order changes its proportions, and exchanges a monumental for a human scale. Hermeses, Atlantises and caryatids of a purely decorative nature become widespread. A light, neutral scale of colours, typical of Russian classical architecture, is replaced by intensive, varied colour schemes which imitate the colouring of the paintings of Pompeii. It is in these ways that an epoch-making building such as the New Hermitage differs from the surrounding older buildings of the Winter Palace complex. Built by N Efimov after the project of a famous German architect, Leo von Klenze (1839-52), the New Hermitage became one of the first large European museums of its type. The contemporary view of the museum as a visual embodiment of

be enlivened by different sorts of flowers as often as possible. Can we find the plucky fellow, the daredevil, who will dare to contrast the flat and the rugged, as they are contrasted in nature when she creates in quick succession the plain, then rocks, cliffs and hills?'

The romantic enthusiasm for the natural, for architectural spontaneity in towns, was combined with the desire to create the semblance of century-old historical stratifications in individual new developments. At the same time, approaches to public spaces changed radically. The classical tendency towards the creation of an elongated chain of vast open squares, most effectively illustrated in Petersburg, became the focus of sharp criticism, which motivated the development of a planning strategy based on denser, more 'spontaneous' building. This reaction fell in line with the intensive style of capitalist building ventures, but it also led to the conscious transformation of squares into public gardens and town parks. The planting of trees and shrubs made significant improvements in the conditions of high-density town centres. The architecture of eclecticism provided a key to the repair of the urban environment – a unifying framework for buildings of different epochs, infill for

FROM LEFT TO RIGHT: SHTAKENSHNEIDER, NIKOLAEVSKY PALACE, ST PETERSBURG, 1853-61; REZANOV, PALACE OF VLADIMIR ALEXANDROVICH, 1867-72

history, a distinctive exhibit absorbing the stylistic features of many periods, was clearly demonstrated in the interior decoration of this building.

The conscious desire for a 'multi-style' approach, which emerges in the museum architecture of the 19th century, also influenced the character of ordinary urban developments. The reaction against the monotonous standardised housing developments of late Russian classicism highlighted the predictable stylistic uniformity of the cities, which was especially apparent in the Petersburg of Nicholas I's reign. The passionate appeal for stylistic diversity was first made in an article by Gogol entitled 'On the Architecture of the Present Time', which became a manifesto of eclecticism in Russia as early as the beginning of the 1830s. He proclaimed: 'A town must consist of diverse shapes and forms, if we want it to give pleasure to people. Let it combine many different tastes. In the same street let the gloomy Gothic rise high, framed by the splendour of oriental decorations and colossal Egyptian forms, and juxtaposed with the regular shapes of Greek architecture. . . . Only occasionally should houses be allowed to merge into one straight monotonous wall, instead of moving back and forth. The streets should

all the empty spaces, decorative vitality and detail throughout. Kiosks, pavilions, bill boards, garden and park railings, benches, lamp-posts and entrance porches multiplied everywhere, and signs of all colours and sizes gradually filled the facades and gave the central streets of large Russian cities that 'urbanistic' quality, which was intensified further by the appearance of the first horse trams, a new type of transport. The increasing density of construction had a significant effect on the volumes and spatial arrangements of buildings – passages, banks, museums, rented housing, and even city palaces. Their structures were set back deep into the site, sometimes with an exit leading out onto the street opposite, similar to the way in which the earliest European alleys were created, by cutting through the midst of medieval blocks.

At the same time, eclecticism involved a visual 'code', so that each different style became linked with a chain of historic and literary associations evoking a different image. In particular, the style of the Renaissance 'palazzo' became widely popular, and its decorative details commonly applied to palaces, banks, and commercial buildings irrespective of their layout, structure, or functional requirements. The development of the composition deep into the site became an idiosyncrasy of large city palaces. The impressive resolutions of their interiors were expressed in a many-tiered net of facades. These characteristics first appeared in the series of Petersburg palaces built for the Tsar by Shtaken-shneider – Mariinsky (1839-44), Nikolaevsky (1853-61), and Novo-Mikhailovsky (1857-61). They combined stylistic features from both housing and public building developments of the eclectic period. The repetition of the same elements – windows, pilasters, a cornice, in both horizontal and vertical directions – enabled the architect to increase the number of floors and the length of the street facades. In this way, houses could be situated on the most inconvenient sites of town, and follow all the curves of the street, thus creating one continuous building line. In this respect the planning concepts of eclecticism were closer to medieval precedents than to the classical. Building began to proliferate on the narrow urban sites, filling vacant spaces and forming the system of courtyards – 'the pits' – which became synonymous with Dostoyevsky's Petersburg.

All these features were clearly displayed in the so-called Vladimir Alexandrovich Palace in Petersburg. Built in 1862–72, it was designed by Alexander Rezanov, Rector of the Academy

nois, 1875), Ribinsk (V Schreter, 1877), and, finally, Odessa, built in 1883-87 by architects F Felner and G Gelmer, winners of an open European competition. In shop architecture, a new kind of *torgovie riadi* (row of shops) similar to the *Verkhnie torgovie riadi* (Upper Shopping Rows) in Moscow (Alexander Pomerantsev, 1849-96), and the main building of the Nizhny Novgorod Fair (Trayman, Trambitsky, Gogen, 1889-90), was developed through the combination of the traditional Russian open arcade with covered, skylit, gallery.

Experimentation in style and layout determined the development of the railway station, in which the basis of composition was the covered platform. Most typical in this respect were the railway buildings by the architect Alexander Krakau, who designed the largest railway station in Petersburg – the Baltic Station (1855-57), and also the Warsaw Station (1858-62) which linked Russia to the railway network of Western Europe.

But along with structural and functional achievements such as these, which were common to historicist architecture throughout Europe, Russian architecture of the second half of the 19th century was distinguished by a particular artistic quest for a modern architecture based on *narodnost*, or national roots. This

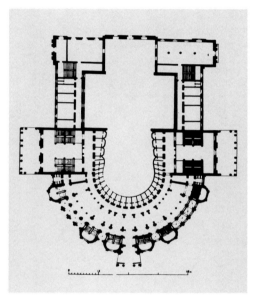

FROM LEFT TO RIGHT: KRAKAU, BALTIC STATION, PETERSBURG, 1855-7; FELNER & GELMER, ODESSA THEATRE, 1884-7, PLAN; NIKITIN, POGODIN IZBA, MOSCOW, 1850s

of Arts and Chairman of the St Petersburg Architectural Society, the first such in Russia. This palace provided the opportunity for many young architects to take part in its construction and, in particular, in its interior decoration. These interiors stand as the visual expression of the creative credo of the eclectic architects. The hall is situated above a light, snow-white staircase which leads deep into the building and is saturated with gilded stucco mouldings; the dark oak panels of the dining room are made in 'Russian style'. All this creates an impression similar to a scenery change in the motion pictures which were fast gaining in popularity at that time. The interiors of the living apartments are completed in a similar but simplified style, suited to their own purposes, whether dining, reclining, or sleeping. Thus stylistic variety is given order by functional clarity. Structural innovations distinguished all types of buildings, firstly the traditional ones such as theatres and commercial buildings, and later museums, railway stations, banks, and exhibition halls. In Russian theatrical architecture, a new layout was developing with the semicircular foyer lapping around the auditorium, on the facade. First introduced by G Zemker, it provided the basis for new theatres in Riga (Victor Shreter, 1877), Pavlovsk (N Be-

had already appeared during the romantic epoch, embracing first Byzantinism, and later Slavophilism. The complexity of the historical situation in Russia at that period was clearly reflected in the country's art and architecture. The antagonism between a growing democratic movement and reactionary protective ideas was basic to the nature of Russian romanticism. The idea of national roots was interpreted in diametrically opposed ways by the art establishment on the one hand, and those democratic tendencies in music, literature, and the plastic arts on the other, which looked towards a revival of the national culture through the creative work of the people.

First attempts at design work in the 'Russian style' had appeared already during the classical period of classicism. In particular, V P Stasov gave to the basically classical churches in Kiev (1826-30) and Potsdam (1827-32) internal decorative features deriving from Old Russian temples of different epochs such as the *zakomora*, and *kokoshnik*. The official Byzantine style, typical of the work of Konstantin Ton, represented a continuation of this tendency. His projects included a number of churches in Petersburg, Moscow, and other Russian towns, for example the Cathedral of Christ the Saviour in Moscow, (1839-

83), as well as large public buildings in the Byzantine style, such as Moscow's Kremlin Palace (1839-49) and Armoury Chamber (1844-50), which form a complicated architectural complex, extending the historical development of the Kremlin; and two architecturally identical railway stations on the former Nicholas Railway in Petersburg and Moscow (1843-51).

A more accurate copying of the Byzantine monuments led to a modification of the official tendency, displayed in the grandiose cathedrals built in Petersburg, Kronstadt and a number of cities in the outlying areas. The Greek Church in Petersburg (1863-66) by Roman Kuzmin, and the cathedral in Hersones (1861-71) by David Grimm, which followed Byzantine originals almost exactly, provided the inspiration for numerous chapels and churches.

In contrast to the official version of the Byzantine style, associated with the particular political complexion of Tsarism, the first examples of wooden architecture began to appear during the romantic epoch. This created the basis for the 'Russian style' of the 19th century. To start with, these structures had the character of peasants' buildings such as might be used for court entertainments. The very few preserved examples show

This movement, which was developed most fully in the work of Victor Gartman and Ivan Ropet, received the warm support of the famous critic V Stasov, who saw in it a direct analogy to the music being composed by the members of the 'Mighty Group'. Though such direct parallels are obviously debatable, there is no doubt that strong links existed between very different fields of art. Thus Gartman's projects and drawings, now the subject of increasing academic attention, were an important inspiration to Mussorgsky in the creation of masterpieces such as *Pictures at an Exhibition*, even though the aesthetic quality of the former could not match up to the genius of the music which they inspired.

Gartman's explorations of architectural form, based on the use of traditional building materials such as wood and brick, were of great importance for the further development of Russian architecture. The boldness of the wooden constructions which he developed was fully appreciated by the time of his death and the dismantling of the exhibition buildings and people's theatre which he designed for the First National Polytechnical Exhibition of 1872 in Moscow.

The building of the Polytechnical Museum provides a lasting

FROM LEFT TO RIGHT: GARTMAN, PROJECT FOR GATES OF KIEV, 1869; MONIGETTI & SHOKHIN, POLYTECHNICAL MUSEUM, MOSCOW, 1870s

that the Russian *izbas* (peasant cottages) in the Alexandrov colony in Potsdam were apparently built to the designs of Ogust Monferron, architect of similar buildings in the Ekaterinofh leisure park in Petersburg several years earlier.

One of the later examples of the Russian *izba* was the house of the famous Slavophile, M P Pogodin, built in the 1850s by Nilkolai Nikitin. This house was the visual embodiment of the ideas underlying the revival of folk traditions and a folk way of life in Russia. It was the forerunner of many wooden buildings in the Russian style, which have since become known as 'pseudo-Russian'. The model was used for the construction of people's schools and *zemstvo* (rural district) hospitals after the Agrarian Reform of 1862 opened the way for capitalism in Russia; and also small railway stations, town and country mansions, and numerous pavilions at the Russian and international industrial exhibitions.

The architecture of the wooden pavilions constituted a synthesis of features typical of the pseudo-Russian style of the 1870s – a combination of new functional and constructional achievements with the traditional decorative forms borrowed from native wooden architecture and folk art.

memento of this exhibition. The earliest part of the museum was built between 1873 and 1877 to the designs of Ippolit Monigetti by the architect Nikolai Shokhin, and represented the first civic example of the Russian style executed in brick. This style was foreshadowed in the first architectural experiments of V Gartman, who had demonstrated the then-new method of brick ornamentation organically incorporated with the wall in a development at Mamontov's printing house in Moscow (1872).

Under the influence of Gartman's works, a special line of eclecticism began to emerge: the so-called 'brick style', which had much in common with Western European developments, and particularly, with the German *Ziegelbau* tendency. Its main feature was the introduction of simplified brick ornamentation into the facades of large brick buildings such as railway stations, educational institutions, hospitals, factories and industrial plants.

Civil and ecclesiastical brick architecture of the 18th century provided models for another retrospective branch of the pseudo-Russian style, connected with the conservationist ideas of the 1880s-1890s. This line exploited the antagonism between classicism and Old-Russian decorative details, as can be appreciated particularly well in the severely symmetrical building, unusual for Old-Russian civil architecture, of the Moscow Duma (Moscow Council) (1890-92), by Dmitri Chichagov. An attempt to escape from the academic severity of classicism was made by V Shervnd in his earlier project for the Historical Museum in Red Square, Moscow (1875-83), where for the first time in a large public building compositional techniques in line with the picturesque structures of the surrounding buildings were used to achieve organic integration of the new with the old.

The most complicated interweaving of apparently incompatible tendencies in the pseudo-Russian style is well illustrated by the first architectural experiments carried out by the artists of the Abramtsevsky Circle. The work of these artists and the personality of Savva Mamontov, owner of Abramtsevo and life and soul of the society, has so far been little explored in spite of its influence on the development of Russian architecture at the end of the 19th and beginning of the 20th century. However this situation is changing. The fact that ordinary artists, least constrained by the stereotypes of the architectural thinking of their time, took the first steps towards the formation of a new imaginative and plastic language in architecture seems very

The trend towards the large organic architectural form, with strong contrasts between huge masses and refined details, marked not only the further work of Polenov and Vasnetsov, but also that of their followers. Artists such as Elena Polenova, Maria Yakunchikova and Konstantin Korovin were all in one way or another connected with the Abramtsevo Circle. Architecture was not the only art form to be affected – so too were book graphics, theatrical set design, and applied art. The adoption of an expressive and formal language from the related plastic arts, combined with a new universalism, led to the realisation of truly innovative architectural achievements by the artists of the circle.

One such example is the Far North Pavilion at the National Artistic and Industrial Exhibition in Nizhny Novgorod, by the artist Korovin, in 1896. This became an important landmark in Russian artistic culture of the time. The architecture of this small pavilion, created under the aegis of Savva Mamontov, the gradation of colour, and a purely plastic formal approach, results in the enhancement of the expressiveness of the mass.

In many respects the artistic achievements of the Abramtsevo Circle paved the way for the architecture of the new century.

FROM LEFT TO RIGHT: ROPET, 'THE CABIN' AT ABRAMTSEVO, 1876; VASNETSOV, 'HUT ON CHICKEN'S LEGS', ABRAMTSEVO, 1883

natural. The first buildings erected in Abramtsevo by Gartman and Ropet, the 'Workshop' and the 'Chamber', which introduced a romantic and figurative element to Abramtsevo Park, provided these artists with their starting point. But while the work of Gartman and Ropet was typically eclectic in style, the Abramtsevo artists went further, developing in their architectural work new methods of artistic stylisation, exaggerating and generalising the conscious aestheticism underlying the main features of the old prototypes.

In the search for new forms and figurative techniques, and a new vision of architecture, those methods of artistic generalisation typical of folk art and Old Russian icon-painting proved a valuable basis. Abramtsevo Church, built to the plans of the artists Vassily Polenov and Victor Vasnetsov in 1881-82, was the first building to display these new features. Polenov's decision to use as his prototype the severe 12th-century temple of Spas Nereditsa was very bold for its time. It was a demonstration of freedom from the official line in architecture, and marked a move towards new plastic resources, which was to enable an organic transition into Modernism at the beginning of the 20th century.

Fedor Shekhtel was one of the first of the new generation of artists to be influenced in this way. His works, such as the Glasgow exhibition pavilions, embody a new understanding of romanticism in architecture. These romantic tendencies stiffened as they came into confrontation with the prosaic character of capitalist architecture, drawing strength from the exploration of plasticity and space which had given life and variety to Russian architecture during the second half of the 19th century.

Until recently, the complicated route taken by Russian architecture, continuing through several decades of the 20th century, has been misinterpreted as an exploration of purely technical questions. In fact the developments of the 19th century resulted in the creation of a stable artistic system, enjoying close links with ideas being generated in other fields of art, and constituting an inseparable part of the overall artistic and cultural structure of the epoch.

Dr Elena Borisova is a Senior Research Fellow of the Institute of Art History, Moscow

THE HISTORICAL MUSEUM
A Moscow design competition 1875-83

Evgenia Kirichenko

EVGENIA KIRICHENKO

VLADIMIR SHERVUD, HISTORICAL MUSEUM, MOSCOW, 1875-83: VIEW FROM RED SQUARE IN 1884

The creation of a museum of Russian history on Red Square in Moscow was one of the most significant building episodes during what we call the Reform Period in Russia, which runs from the Emancipation of the Serfs in 1861 to the first, bourgeois, Revolution of 1905. It was a period not just of politics, but of historical investigation of Russia itself, and of deep questioning of the proper nature and subject of history as an idea. Amidst the general questioning of classical canons in Russia, and their increasingly strong identification with the lack of political freedom, the documentation which has survived on the design and execution of this project reflects those larger concerns with particlar clarity, and shows us some concrete examples of how different approaches in those areas were correlated to particular architectural forms.

The project for what is now called The Historical Museum began when a foundation stone was laid by Tsar Alexander II on 20 August 1875, and ended, from our point of view, with the opening of the first eleven halls by Alexander III on 27 May 1883. Its aim was the typically 19th-century one, as the 'Programme of the Museum' Stated, of 'making visual the history of the main epochs of the Russian State'. It was thus to be a visual embodiment of the events and characteristics which identified Russia as a nation, and that was the conceptual loading which designers must express in the look of the building. By conviction many considered this must be a style derived from medieval or vernacular architecture. But amidst the diversity of Russia's architectures, which one? To others the argument for a 'Russian' style was contextual. The site cleared for the Museum was at the north end of Red Square, immediately outside the Kremlin walls and close to the next defensive line, then still extant, of the Kitaigorod wall. St Basil's cathedral stood at the south end, and the museum site itself abutted the ancient Iverskaia Gate. All were medieval and predominantly brick.

These factors produced a rare unanimity on the Construction Committee that the style must be 'Russian', but argument began when it came to designating the periods or specific buildings which offered proper models. The Committee contained well-known architects, among them Lev Dal and Vladimir Shervud

who would enter the competition themselves, and two well-known historians, A S Uvarov and I E Zabelin, whose arguments dominated the process of drawing up the building programme.

As historians these two belonged to opposed schools. Thus when Uvarov said that the Museum should be modelled stylistically on 12th-century cathedrals of Vladimir-Suzdal and Andrei Bogoliubov's nearby palace, whilst Zabelin proposed the 16th-century St Basil's and its 17th-century legatees around Moscow, it was the statist view of history being opposed to the populist.

The heritage of Vladimir-Suzdal derived from the period of competition and conquest between regional principalities that led to a unified Russian State, and for centuries it had been a symbol of autocracy and the pretention to great-power status. The related Assumption cathedral in the Kremlin had the same connotations. To Zabelin this architecture was still inherently Roman in principle. His advocacy of St Basil's derived from his adherence to the 'archaeological' school of Russian historiography. In that view the historical process was not interpreted in terms of the directive role of the State; the structure and character of that State were determined by the way of life and the spiritual concepts of the people, of the peasant mass, and given their illiteracy, these fields were investigated through the remains of their material culture, namely through archaeology.

For Zabelin the key structuring principle in that culture was the patriarchal one, which when magnified to the national scale became the ideal of political unity. The radial-concentric form of Moscow itself was an embodiment of this idea, 'dominant and primary in our private life and thence transmitted across Russian soil … It grew and developed by expressing the populist idea of political unity in each circle of its plan and its fortress walls.'[1] That centralised, patriarchal character found its highest expression in St Basil's, itself erected at the centre of the whole plan. Architecturally, Zabelin saw it as the peak of a centuries-long process of increasing sophistication in the assemblage of basic elements whose origins lay in the life-style of pre-Christian Russia: the simple cubic cell or *kletka* of logs which was the peasant *izba*, with its varieties of roof and elaboration in the facetted, tent-shaped *shatior*, the conical *kolpak*, the bonnet-shaped *bochka*.

In Zabelin's architectural genealogy, these elements of the human house naturally became the elements of God's house when Russia adopted Christianity. Their eventual transformation into a stone and brick architecture in the 16th century coincided with the final achievement of a unified Russian State – the very event celebrated by the construction of St Basil's, which Zabelin saw as incorporating 'the unique features of this people'.[2]

On contextual grounds, even Uvarov was prepared to accept the primary role of St Basil's as a model in the competition. Thus the programme was effectively a reflection of Zabelin's views. V O Shervud and A A Semionov, who had worked on the preliminary project, were joined by six other architects in the competition, but their headstart won them the commission.

Shervud's accompanying notes are of great interest for their explicitness about his particular interpretations of the generally populist argument on both history and style, which in many respects differ diametrically from Zabelin's.

Where Zabelin, for example, saw individual forms as the embodiment of populist historical values and the basic subject matter of aesthetics, Shervud placed the emphasis on rules and modes of composition. In his view, Zabelin's focus on the individual structural element absolutised the private, rather than the corporate. It therefore prevented the building from 'showing either the elevated nature of the Russian spirit or its constancy, or indeed the courage, the magnaminity, the self-confidence of Russian culture, its Christian foundations or intellectual and commercial sides – in a word all of it.'[3]

Shervud presented the results of his research into Russian architecture in the form of an explanatory note, stating the compositional laws which seemed to him to be the determining characteristics of Russian architecture, and hence the essence of its 'nationalness'. His six 'laws' of Russian composition ran thus: '1: The building consists of several parts differentiated by height and position but comprising one indivisible whole. 2: The grouping of those parts of the building which significantly project or rise above the rest must approximate a conical form. 3: The grouping of parts is such that all are interconnected, so that from all points of view the various parts form a unified overall composition with nothing appearing alienated or separated from the whole. 4: A look of stability is achieved by the fact that the overall mass and its parts have the general proportions of a square … 5: There is a strong use of line in the delineation of form, expressed through elements such as cornices, and banding. 6: The general treatment of the building and its parts is characterised by diversity.'[4] Whilst they might differ in their emphasis, both Zabelin and Shervud insisted upon deep knowledge of forms and their historical origins. Equally, both of them maintained the grandiose aspiration that their work and the application of their ideas whould create a genuinely national character in Russia's future architecture.

Shervud's comparisons between the Russian medieval styles and the European Gothic are also revealing, and re-emphasise his concern for the spiritual dimension. Thus the essence of Russian character was defined by that he called 'the breadth of the Russian style'. Its medieval architecture 'contains the good sides of the Gothic, which are its elevatedness and lightness, but it also has breadth, which is lacking in the Gothic.'[5] Gothic's exaggerated emphasis on the vertical was a reflection of the one-sidedness of Catholicism, said Shervud. Catholicism understood elevatedness egotistically, as personal salvation. 'Only the Orthodox church has achieved a full understanding of the Christian idea. The Catholic church expresses absolute will; the Protestant, reason; the Orthodox, the feeling of great Christian love.'[6] In marked contrast to Catholic and Protestant, 'the Russian representatives of the spiritual and moral idea elevate the spirit as a force capable of active influence among people and capable of bringing universal good.'[7] This orthodox notion of the essential spirituality of daily life and all human affairs was the unique feature of the Russian peasantry, the *narod*, which made it simultaneously a model for all mankind. Herein lay 'the true source of a genuine cosmopolitanism, and in the sacred love for humanity lies the supreme unifying force'.[8]

This focus upon the communion rather than the individual soul led Shervud to take the church, and not the *izba*, as the basis for his architectural principles. In the next step he extended the populist idea of the Russian people's destiny to effect a moral transformation of humanity into the conviction of a great future for Russian architecture. Thus he wrote in his book of 1895, on *Investigations into the Laws of Art*, which elaborated these relationships between historiography, culture and aesthetics, that 'The Russian people are fated to be the bearers of the pure Christian idea which will restore the fullness and all-sidedness of the manifestation of the spiritual idea in architecture.'[9]

In the exterior of the Historical Museum he reflected this vision on two levels. First, from the contextual point of view stressed by Uvarov. Second, through emphasis on 'architecture of an ecclesiastical character … to express clearly the fact that the church was not just a holy idea in our people's history, but also the main cultural element of our nation' whose 'historic relics and remains' the Museum was destined to house.[10]

From the Kremlin he drew the formal notion of peripherally distributed towers around a body that is relatively unfragmented, with its references to a notion of the 'sacred city' of Jerusalem. By Zabelin's standards the volumetric building blocks were far too closely congealed: the *kletki, bochki* and *shatiory* are there, but he condemned the result as 'unscientific' and far too 'Gothic' or even 'Moslem' in character. The tall corner towers, in particular, 'recall Mohamedan minarets and give it the flavour of a Mohamedan or even Catholic temple.'[11]

Whereas the exterior represented the national ideal of generality, Shervud's approach to the interiors was concrete.

The planning of the first rooms seems today excessively complex, as it diverges from the normal enfiladed sequence. But its geometry and the choices of route are a precise model of the historical relationships of the diverse cultures it presents, just as light, form, colour and decorative treatment derive directly from these.

Thus two doorways lead from the entrance hall. One leads into a sequence on the Stone and Bronze Ages and the early Slavonic periods; the other into the early Christian rooms. They flow together again into the Kiev room, as ancient language groups and the earliest Christianity in Russia became united in the culture and political domain of the Kievan Russ under Prince Vladimir. This period was followed by renewed fragmentation, broadly a bifurcation, on the new axes of Vladimir-Suzdal and Novgorod-Pskov. Thus two exits lead from the Kiev room, through parallel sequences which re-unite, never to divide again, in the first rooms of the Moscow period. Thus the historical flow-diagram is written into the visitor's itinerary.

Short-lived periods of cultural fragmentation were represented by small rooms; semi-darkness pervades the Time of Troubles, whereas light floods out of the Christian room. The roofing enclosure to each pace represented the constructive basis of its architecture. Thus in the Ancient Russian rooms the ceiling was vaulted; in the hall of Ancient Chrisitan art it was cupola-shaped; for Greek settlements of the Black Sea coast it was flat beams; in the hall of Hellenistic and Scythian monuments it was corbelled on the model of their Pantheistic tombs.

ROOM OF GREEK COLONIAL CULTURES IN 1883

ROOM OF THE KIEVAN RUSS IN 1883

From the Paleolithic period, represented by great murals by Victor Vasnetsov, right through the rest, wall-paintings of life-style and the popular historical experience were backdrops to decorative treatments of the architectural features which derived directly from the craftwork and vernacular building of that culture.

In general Shervud handled these Museum interiors as he would have handled any other 'style' interior, and in this synthesis of idea and form one sees a reflection of thinking at that time. The difference here is in the primacy of documentary accuracy, as an element of the educative armoury and the aspiration to communicate historical information – or rather a historical view – which is the *raison d'être* of the Museum. In a sense it is like a 'national pavilion' at some international exhibition writ large: there is a pre-established story-line which architectural forms must communicate. As an attitude to the museum type it is culturally specific: nationalist in purpose and therefore contrasting with the internationalism expressed by most 'national museums' of the late 19th century through classicism. This one is manifestly egalitarian in its value system, in the level at which it addresses its public. It has that role of 'leading its public

forward', the *veduiushyi* role, which was always central to Realism and would equally animate Socialist Realism. The semantics here, however, are explicitly and intentionally local. The Renaissance palazzo, the Baroque palace, spoke the language of a system of ideas that was culturally widespread. Classicism thus retained comprehensibility across a vast geographical area. The Historical Museum is a good example of the way in which a truly regional architecture requires commentary if the cultural outsider is to understand its symbolism.

1 Zabelin, *Studies in Russian Antiquity and History*, II, Moscow, 1873, pp 109, 140
2 Zabelin, *Ancient Russian Art*, Moscow, 1900, p110
3 Historical Museum, Written Documents Dept, f 440, e 110, p 32
4 Historical Museum, Written Documents Dept, e 276, Explanatory Notes on the Project ... 1876
5 Historical Museum, Written Documents Dept, e 110, p 31
6 Shervud, *Some Notes Concerning the Historical Museum*, Moscow, 1879, p 19
7 Shervud, *Investigations into the Laws of Art*, Moscow, 1895, p 129
8 Shervud, *Some Notes*, p 24
9 Shervud, *Investigations*, p 126
10 Explanatory Notes, p 235
11 Historical Museum, Written Documents Dept, e 278, pp 120-1; e 275, p12

Dr Evgenia Kirichenko is a Senior Research Fellow of the Institute of Art History, Moscow

THE SUZDAL ROOM IN 1883

THE VLADIMIR ROOM IN 1883

AN EXCHANGE OF OPINIONS
Soviet architects from various republics discuss

I: TRADITION AND MODERNITY

National in the Contemporary

Margarita Astafeva-Dlugach (*Moscow*)

The pursuit of national individuality is not a new concern for architecture. Nor is it a new approach within Soviet architecture itself. From the beginning of the 1930s, after the first post-Revolutionary reconstructions of our creative affairs were over, Soviet architecture started to address the problem of 'assimilating the heritage' of its many different nationalities and cultures. During the next two decades the attempt to find a synthesis of architectural traditions with new social and technological possibilities generated a number of theoretical principles to underpin most important processes taking place in our architecture.

At that date however there was a very conspicuous gulf between the theoretical propositions of the leading Soviet architects and the ways in which these principles of assimilating the heritage were actually being realised. In an article entitled 'Arguable Questions' in the *Literary Gazette*, Alexander Vesnin wrote of this phenomenon in 1934: 'Attempts at assimilation of the architectural heritage are producing objects that are completely absurd. The majority of architects approach the historical heritage of architecture like a chest full of drawers, each pulling out of it what he fancies and sticking it onto his project. Neither architects nor critics understand that the old architecture has to be included in the new disassembled form.'

Since then Soviet architecture has travelled a long way and developed many new ideas, but there is good reason for suggesting that many principles worked out in the 1930s and never then fully realised in built works are now beginning to come to fruition.

The architects working on this problem, complex as it is in both aesthetic and the ethical respects, are beginning to appreciate the national heritage not merely at the level of its individual forms or details, but also at the more profound level of the underlying architectural principles.

What then do we understand by national characteristics in architecture? There are many sorts of architectural nationalism, but I shall discuss only the two which I see as the most distinctive.

The first is that which seeks to exploit the potential of those specific architectural features which arise the aesthetic traditions and the life-style of the people concerned, their psychology, the climatic conditions of their environment and so on. These features are relatively stable and usually widely acknowledged.

The second approach is that which actually subverts and undermines the traditions underlying the historical development of national architecture, setting up a new style of building which now their descendants would interpret as particularly characteristic of that country's. This is precisely what happened in Russian architecture of the 18th and early 19th centuries. The architects themselves were convinced that they were being internationalist, working within a current that was common to the whole of Europe. In the end, however the particular brand of classicism which they created came to be regarded as national architecture specific to Russia.

Opposite as these approaches seem, they have much in common, for a national architecture is not created by the forces of one particular period or by one single creative act – it is built up in space and consciousness over time. The implications of this truth are also important for our own period.

The approach of the 1930s was based primarily on the application of surface details which were simple to perceive and made the most obvious connection in the public mind between the architecture and a particular people or region. Now our approach is closer to what Vesnin called inclusion of the old in the

VYSOTIN, GULISTAN CENTRE, ASHKHABAD, 1981

new 'in disassembled form'. Direct, even documentarily precise copying of certain images is being abandoned in favour of a more generalised treatment of form, which gives it a contemporary resonance. Thus free play with the forms of Doric columns, enables the designers of Ashkhabad's new Gulistan shopping centre to remind us that this area was once ruled by a Hellenistic Parthenon. Designers of the big new tourist centre in the ancient city of Suzdal used a series of subtle formal association to make manifest the Russian architectural parentage of an entirely contemporary building. In a manner particularly sensitive to the general roofscape of the town the *shatior* (tent-shaped) tower of the restaurant is erected in Suzdal's traditional materials of white stone, timber and bronze, which blend naturally with the ancient churches and double-pitched roofs of the other buildings.

Also becoming widespread is the direct quotation of a specific prototype, or the inclusion of genuine fragments of something original within reconstructed buildings. This latter approach was the key to success at the new Taganka theatre complex in Moscow, which shows a refined appreciation of the palette and tactile values typical of indigenous historical architecture, which in Moscow means the use of red brick.

The overt respect for historical imagery which these new buildings represent is important, because with us, as elsewhere, such thinking has sometimes been fiercely derided. But in evaluating our own time we must not forget those other buildings, finished or under construction, which our successors will regard as equally genuine products of an identifiably 'national' architecture, but to us merely seem like good modern buildings.

The live traditions of Russian architecture

Andrei Ikonnikov (*Moscow*)

The architecture of Russia – what is it? Such has been the territorial and historical role of the Russian people within the USSR that problems of national tradition are generally posed as problems of the non-Russian cultures. There are reasons of history and social psychology behind this, but the result has been a watering down of the specificity of Russian architecture which, given Russia's central role, has tended to misdirect the focus of all Soviet architecture away from deeper characteristics towards the exotic detail.

That said, it has to be admitted that one impediment to a clear characterisation of Russian architecture is its own diversity. The country which is Russia today did itself start out as an assembly of different, indeed rival, national cultures. Thus we have a precise white-stone architecture from the Suzdal area; we have picturesque and formally very simplified architecture from Pskov; we have the rougher, wilder architecture of early 18th-century Moscow, and equally the strict harmonies of St Petersburg. What they have in common is a spatial environment, and it is to this tradition that we must look for the unifying factors. A tradition which reinforces this, both historically and now, is that of a strong adherence to standardised buildings. The 'type solution' inevitably creates the impression of buildings that exist in a somewhat abstracted space. The outcome is that design is a matter of what is done with the site, of how buildings are arranged to create an environment. In the city, the decisive problem is that of the overall spatial environment.

This brings us to the question of how 'international' styles like classicism became 'Russian'. Here St Petersburg is a typical and illuminating example. The city was developed initially on the basis of medieval models of Russian town planning, in which a city core of key ensembles form a kind of 'island' amidst spaces designated for a low, flat perimeter development. We see this model clearly in Russian medieval towns such as Moscow, Yaroslavl, Novgorod, Suzdal, Tobolsk, Tiumen and many others. In Petersburg, that 'island' was formed of two main cores on opposite sides of the river: the Peter and Paul fortress and the Admiralty. Onto their verticals was focused a system of radial streets lined by buildings on the rural principle of ample spacing. Only later was the conventional approach of classicism applied, with vast streets developed as continuous single facades. The principles underlying the original spatial structure were thus entirely traditional ones, despite the modern, internationalist air of the architecture of individual elements.

If we speak honestly, we have to admit that professional levels of sophistication and competence with respect to the urban environment are not very high at the moment. At last, however, there are signs that this essentially Russian focus on overall composition is being rescued from oblivion. We look with joy at what is currently being achieved in ancient Vladimir, where the environment as a whole is at last being given proper consideration. Likewise in Sverdlovsk. We need to refocus attention the intermediate spaces which provide the living fabric between the intimate domestic ones.

In relation to the use of the historical vernacular, another problem arises, because in general the art-historical literature on this subject focuses on ornament, or at best on the sculptural characteristics of the structures. Inherent to the vernacular, but now neglected,

ZEMTSOV ET AL, NEVSKY MARKET, 1983

was also the traditional wisdom concerning the site location and internal organisation of settlements. In ancient Slavic settlements, for example, we have centroidal ring planning; on steep sloping sites in Dagestan, the 'carpet' pattern of development. Such solutions evolve out of the specific ways in which life-functions are organised in space. And in our own consideration of this question we must not only recognise the historically valid constants, but also appreciate the effect of change. For the interrelationship between old and new forms the social content of our lives. We build administrative buildings without any clear thinking about how a Soviet office may differ from an American one, say. Leonidov, in the 1920s, starting thinking about this, but no-one since then has bothered to give it serious attention.

In respect of the social organisation of space, as with technical questions, one thing is clear. Static conservation would be anti-traditional. Our historical towns have been enriched by the new at all stages of their development. We need to take our prototypes and rework them, as the new Nevsky Market in Leningrad, for example, has been designed along the lines of the Gostiny Dvor. By this path we could return to the positive traditions of standardised buildings which we have foolishly forgotten, with all the emphasis they create on pattern and use of the spaces between.

National and Regional in the Architecture of Uzbekistan

Shurkur Askarov (*Uzbekistan*)

Within any one republic of the Soviet Union today there is a diversity of views on the issue of the vernacular, and design approaches to the problem of establishing a dialogue with that history may be diametrically opposed. To demonstrate our belief in the productiveness of discussion, I present here a brief account of a session we held in Tashkent from 3-6 June last summer on the theme of 'The national and the regional in the architecture of Uzbekistan', under the chairmanship of Professor Iuri Bocharov, Director of the Central Institute for the History and Theory of Architecture in Moscow. The main papers were given by myself, as chairman of the 'Architectural theory and criticism' committee of the Uzbekistan Union of Architects, and by the deputy chairman Dr I I Notkin, whose comments I shall present first.

I I NOTKIN: Although we do have a solid theoretical platform from which to approach certain aspects of this problem, there still re-

main a lot of open questions demanding much more theoretical and experimental design work. The areas most in need of further definition, from my point of view, are two: the discussion of how we can distinguish what is 'positive' or 'progressive' in our historical legacy from what is reactionary and outdated, and the attempts to make a direct connection between architectural theory and building practice. Here in Uzbekistan we have become dispirited by the gulf which has developed between the readiness of the republic's research and design institutes in Tashkent to improve the aesthetic quality of mass housing developments, and the meagre assortment of components actually produced by the industrialised building concerns. For over 15 years all major architectural conferences which have touched on the preservation of our inherited environment have consistently recommended that each city have its conservation areas; its areas of limited redevelopment; that it should work out designs for low-rise housing built out of modern materials and to constructional systems which take account of local life-style and demography. Our own experimental projects have demonstrated that housing of mixed height, at one to four storeys, can compete very favourably on economic grounds with mass-produced housing of a uniform four storeys. And this year, at last, such work has been included in the proposals for the experimental and standard design catalogue of Uzbekistan's State building organisation, Gosstroi UzSSR, and we are collaborating with them. The aim is to bring the inhabitants of our region closer to ground level through differentiated building heights, but there are still many obstacles in the way. The chief of these is inertia – mental inertia, which has created innumerable documents laying down norms and regulations.

SH D ASKAROV: The time has finally come when we must recognise that the methods we are utilising to enhance the aesthetic and architectural individuality of our towns generally derive from methods and even images which are applied too uniformly across the whole Soviet Union. The role of republican institutes in this work has been reduced to one of providing information merely as a starting point for otherwise centralised work. The results thus emerge as a national 'average' which cannot solve the specific problems of any particular region. It is only to be expected that design research organised to produce these blanket nationwide standards has disappointingly little influence on reshaping regional cities.

We have an old saying which runs: 'There is only one way to get flowers, which is to grow them'. Herein lies the proper meaning of regionalisation, in both its organisation and its content.

At present the town is at the mercy of diverse and often conflicting planning activity. Even in the integrated research and analysis programmes intended as the basis for real building work up till the end of the century, socially important architectural and planning work is scattered amongst different institutes, between which there is no coordination. At one of the recent plenums of the board of the Union of Soviet Architects there was talk of the necessity for creating a unified centre for methodological and design-orientated research in our field. But in the present situation even this is inadequate. We need to find ways and forms of creating regional centres connected to that national centre, which would be concerned with architecture and town planning, for example in Central Asia. They would aim to bring together the resources of local teams, which are growing but up till now are ineffectively used and are excluded from contributing to research at the national level.

M AKHMEDOV, lecturer in the Samarkand State Architectural and Building Institute: Approaches to this problem in recent years have developed in three different directions.

The first aims to identify and utilise the progressive traditions of the past in the organisation of the spatial environment, seeking to respond to natural, climatic and technological factors as well as the social and ethnographic characteristics of the population. The second operates by quoting forms and motifs from the past without any particular justification or need, and is an approach which can only alarm us. The third direction seeks to intensify the emotional interaction of architecture with the population by applying decorative motifs to nationally available standard projects (often high-rise apartment buildings). Whilst these motifs are often much loved by the population, their application as decorative pseudo solar-protection screens on high-rise buildings cannot be a solution to the problem of national character in architecture. Despite frequent criticism, methods like this are still in increasingly common use.

T D MEMETOVA, departmental director in the Tashkent Zonal Research Institute for Experimental Design: In the literature up till now we find very various understandings of the meaning of 'regional' and 'national' in this context, and of their relationship. We ourselves have been guilty of sanctioning this muddle by careless use of these terms.

The regional represents the geographical datum which in architecture means the patterns of adaptation to climatic conditions, and the character of the natural terrain. The national dimension on the other hand is a set of responses to social phenomena.

The situation today is typified by the universal presence of a level of culture which is international, and we have to take that on board, for the person who has no mastery of that international element of a culture is now hopelessly left behind by the contemporary world. But to humanise the environment, we have to make manifest the genuinely national features of culture within that international context.

In the technical aspects of building architects have fallen behind in developing principles of regional adaptation. These need to be formulated not only as forms of some kind, but given the force of law in the region concerned, for in the end only this can have a sufficiently brutal effect on the whole conduct of building work.

A V MASLOV, leader of the Moscow design office Mosproekt-2: The theme we are examining here is a world problem, part of an

often unrecognised movement to reflect regionality of life-style, philosophy, religious belief, modes of thinking in all aspects of culture and the arts.

The particular character of Central Asian architecture seems to me to be its concern with the whole environment. In Samarkand or Bukhara there is a danger of the individual monuments distracting us from the whole city. Khiva is therefore a better object of study here, as a city where the fixity of architectural stereotypes and modes is so great that the whole town represents one indivisible bit of environment, and whose value therefore lies not in the features of any particular building but in the inseparability of space from time. This is something of great value which in my view demands absolute protection.

Such an environment develops through the operation of a limiting set of canons or rules. These are an exact parallel with the quatrains of Omar Khayam, where an idea is developed, accentuated in the third line in order to return to it in original form in the fourth. That is how our architecture operates: within the limits of the boundaries given, it develops endless diversity of ideas and feelings.

Travelling around Central Asia I see with bitterness how so much that was specific in our national thinking has been literally overwhelmed by a process of internationalisation. To me the best prototype for the future is offered by the architect O P Aidinova's experimental monolithic housing complex, Tashkent's Lenin Boulevard. It is an exploration of the desire of one citizen to create an environment which is intermediary between the individual and the city.

The true and the superficial approach to historical traditions

Reflections on the experience of contemporary Armenian architecture

Artsvin Grigorian & Levon Babaian (*Armenia*)

Tradition is not architectural forms, not building types, not systems of settlement, although it is embodied in all three of these. Tradition is the system of concepts and attitudes evolved in the course of long periods under the influence of diverse factors. These concepts are socially,

ISRAELIAN, MEMORIAL COMPLEX, SARDARABAD, 1979

regionally and nationally determined, and find themselves under constant change. At each stage of development the past reveals new and unpredictable aspects of its continuities. All we can say is that the greater the proportion of innovative trends, the more the 'bridges' between the contemporary world and the past spread out to reveal the great complexities of this continuity.

In Armenian architecture today there coexist diverse stylistic trends. One is a certain tendency towards technicism, where the interests of the functional and technological solution dominate in the form-making process. Aesthetic criteria reflect this, and decorative devices reside in the volumetric and spatial compositions themselves, in the handling of formal considerations, of relative colour both externally and internally. There is a conscious tendency towards exaggeration and deliberate coarsening of forms, towards their juxtaposition in relationships of maximum contrast.

The Russian cinema offers an example of the compositional trends manifesting themselves now, when there exist so many diverse and equally appropriate constructional systems, in particular for covering large spans. When 'technology can do anything', the unlimited possibilities for constructive expression in composition produce the paradoxical situation where the explosion of constructional possibilities has weakened and even eliminated their influence on form. The influence of non-structural and, in particular, aesthetic factors grows, and this in turn leads in too many cases to a love of formal originality at the expense of functional and technological requirements on the building. This in itself is a sign of the times.

The second trend, increasingly widespread in Armenia as elsewhere in recent years, is the examination of national traditions. Those characteristics which are usually attributed to Armenian architecture – a truthfulness in the expression of function and construction, a unity of form and volumes with the architectural organisation of the interior, the use of natural building materials and integrated elements of applied art – are all characteristics of the best architectural work in any nation. In artificially creating the illusion that these are some special creative aspiration of the contemporary generation of Armenian architects, we are departing from the genuinely scientific analysis of practice and are certainly not helping its development.

The task of architectural theorists is to evaluate the stylistic characteristics of today's architecture objectively. Meanwhile the pages of the specialist press are filled with material about Post-Modernism. Why on earth are we so preoccupied with the fate of this trend and hurrying 'to show how educated we are'. We are surrounded by discussions of how the traditional and the national must be reproduced 'with a smile', 'with allusion', 'referentially', with clear recollection – all of which will supposedly link the consciousness of the past with the present.

Such a conception of the role of national specificity has nothing in common with the organic fusion of tradition and innovation when the image, the architectural form, is created from the inside outwards. And its external formal characteristics are the reflection, in all levels of form and content, of the unity of national and international. These 'allusions' and jokes can already be observed in many towns of our country. They ought merely to remind us that we have no right to be ignoring the experience of organically solving these problems which have been built up during the last decades in the various republics of this country, amongst them Armenia, where this process began to take place as far back as the 1920s under the leadership of such architects as Tamanian. And today it is not inappropriate to rethink our own modern history from this point of view.

Ukrainian architecture: history and contemporary development

Vladimir Nikitin (*Ukraine*)

Ukrainian architecture has an extremely dynamic and rich history, distinguished by such achievements as the Ukrainian Baroque, the timber vernacular and church architecture, the famous Constructivist complex for Gosprom in Kharkov and the post-war revival of Ukrainian decorativeness and urban scale in Kiev's broad Kreshchatka. It is a dynamism born of the region's historical and geographical situation and the diversity of cultures which interacted with the traditions of medieval Russian architecture on its territory.

The resulting three-dimensional development of Ukrainian towns has reflected the rich cross-fertilisation of ideas in stylistic and volumetric combinations of great diversity. The inauguration of mass industrialised housing programmes in the 1960s and 1970s somewhat levelled out this diversity and intensified the aspiration to give national characteristics some expression. Thus the 1980s have seen the appearance of a series of distinct architectural trends, or schools, orientated both towards new readings of Functionalism, as in Dnepropetrovsk, and towards national ethnographic motifs, as in Ivanovo-Frankovsk.

Much of the pressure for this latter trend is the consequence of the widespread reconstruction work undertaken in the centres of historic cities. Thus redevelopment projects for the Podol district of Kiev, an area with a thousand-year history and a unique three-dimensional structure and lifestyle, generated lively public discussion about Kiev's architecture in general and the history of Podol district in particular. Projects for redeveloping the Kreshchatka produced even greater reverberations. The Kreshchatka is the city's principal artery, dating mainly from the post-war rebuilding of the ruined city. The actual architecture of this period, which has long been ignored amongst professional historians, became the object of intensive attention. That was good, unfortunately the attention is currently devoted more to the Baroque richness of forms and the freedom of compositions than to the unique compositional and spatial structure of the street and its rich relief with clear relationship of nodes, pauses and dominants.

A further stimulus to elucidating the specificities of Ukrainian architecture has been the extensive work lately concluded on 'A composite listing of historical and cultural monuments of the Ukrainian Republic'. In the

GOLTS, PROJECT FOR KRESHCHATKA, 1944

course of this, hundreds of historical examples of planning were revealed and investigated, as well as architectural monuments. One of the most positive results has been to redirect the search for individual character away from detailed architectural features onto wider characteristics of vernacular settlements. The new situation which has developed in the country today encourages us to rethink the interconnections between democratism and identity, to make diversity of a kind always typical of Ukrainian architecture the basic phenomenon of a new democratism in large-scale housing developments.

On the path to a synthesis

Rustan Karimov (*Tadzhikistan*)

Territorially, Central Asia is a distinctive area of some coherence, and it is accurate enough to see its architecture as characterised today by a strong focus on its vernacular origins. We live with the tourist stereotype in which Central Asia equals Samarkand, Bukhara and Khiva, but it has nothing in common with the real diversity of towns in the four Central Asian republics. Tadzhikistan alone ranges from blazing desert to deep permafrost, from sea-level to the highest mountains of the Pamir. Differences in customs, traditions, living conditions and building materials have produced commensurate differences in the vernacular architectures. The clay structures which the world identifies with this region, for example, exist only in certain parts of Tadzhikistan and Uzbekistan, and the building material in mountain regions is stone.

When the vernaculars became swamped by industrialised uniformity, some old Tadzhik towns like the beautiful Khodzhent, now Leninabad, managed to preserve individuality amidst their standard microdistricts, The capital Dushanbe, on the other hand, was created in the 1920s out of a small village or *kishlak* by architects from European Russia, since the republic itself then had no trained personnel. Neither architecture nor planning had much connection with local Tadzhik practices, and there have been repeated attempts to give it some 'national' character ever since. Nationalistic decoration has a role in this, but only that which it always had, of enhancing, under-

lining, strengthening aspects of the overall image and form created by more properly architectural means. Our problem today is, what should those means be? And to what extent should different building types properly bear some load of 'nationalness' in their architecture?

We see it as important to differentiate here. At one extreme, what is the point of camouflaging an industrial plant of international type under a cloak of 'nationalness'? We see none. At the other, there are buildings which have national flavour by their very type: for us these are museums and exhibition halls, archives of ancient manuscripts, schools and workshops for applied arts, tea houses, bazaars, traditional bath-houses.

Housing comes between the two, but in times of social change it is highly problematic. Which traditions are already broken, and inappropriate to revive as architectural forms? Age-old traditions of strong family ties, of hospitality and conversation, were supported in the dwelling structure by special guest rooms, shady courtyards. If we now revive the courtyard on some floors of a multi-storey housing block, how much of this lifestyle remains? It is a sociological fact that the young want to remain in proximity to their families, but pursue a totally independent lifestyle. So we need careful study of these changes, and housing with a new, multi-variant structure in which links and separations of accommodation can easily be changed. By that means we could genuinely move forward with those aspects of tradition that remain valid.

Assimilation of the heritage is not an aspiration to the archaic

Thoughts of one of the Soviet Union's oldest architects

Mikael Useinov (*Azerbaidzhan*)

I have been working in architecture since the 1930s and can affirm from my own experience that the industrialisation of building and the possibilities opened up by new building materials do not narrow the opportunities for establishing a national identity in architecture. On the contrary, they widen them. They demand that we penetrate deeper into the sense of the pheno-mena concerned, and of a genuinely innovative approach.

What we see worldwide now, as well as here, are various fundamentally different approaches. They range from a near-nihilistic insistence that any such historical influence must be negative, to the mechanical, industrialised reproduction of architectural forms which were satisfactory in relation to the technologies of their time, and have genuinely long-lasting aesthetic value, but are totally out-of-place in the architecture of a modern building. I see no long-term prospects for a constructive dialogue between levels of consciousness and creativity. The task of our time is to formulate new principles appropriate to our age and its materials.

In the Azerbaidzhan republic vernacular architecture has recently been receiving the study it deserves, and has started to influence

REVAZOV ET AL, EASTERN BAZAAR, BAKU, 1978-82

work on restoring the seriously ruined monuments of medieval Baku and Nakhichevani. We are now turning attention to other historic towns, notably Sheki and Ordubad. These are both interesting for the fact that they have preserved their own planning structure and extensive areas of vernacular building, as well as individual architectural masterpieces. We have already well understood that the town as a whole has to be a category within the concept of 'a cultural monument', being in fact the greatest and most synthetic example of any nation's spiritual and material culture. The idea is easy to express – as many people are doing these days – but far more difficult to realise.

Under the conditions prevailing in the Soviet Union today, rural building programmes offer a wide canvas for the pursuit of interesting solutions to the use of traditional and vernacular architectures. The design of rural housing and in particular collective farm villages are at the centre of attention in Uzbekistan as they are within the Soviet architectual community as a whole. Rural building of the past resulted from an extended process of development akin to natural selection, and that realisation in itself should stop us expecting change or success to be achieved too rapidly.

The 'national' house and contemporary mass housing

Gul-Jamal Konduchalova & Igor Likhterov (*Kirgizia*)

The real problem of our mass housing is that is breaks with 'tradition' all too rarely. The area of application considered by those who wrote the Athens Charter was the globe. The practices of recent decades have disregarded geography, so the abstract stereotype of a 'correct' organisation of the dwelling and the town, considered uniquely 'right for all', is not concretely correct for anyone.

'Loving humanity is easy', says the old adage, 'loving one's neighbour is much harder'. The Athens Charter dealt successfully with the first half of this judgement; we however have to deal with the second part. Today as never before the unbroken link between the human being and the whole of existence on earth is important, beginning with his link to those

alongside him. Everyone must turn to face his neighbour.

The International Style remains something valid only in the inter-spaces between nations. In reaction against it has arisen the perfectly explicable desire to establish self-identity, demonstrated by the upsurge of popular interest in history, to experience participation in the world at the most personal level – through the home, the family, the wider kinship group, and the native country. We have the desire to establish a genetic connection with the past and to restore some integrated picture of the world at the level of the individual.

The dissatisfaction with today's state of affairs in the field of housing and the city has been generated by many factors, but it began with a wider malaise of spiritual purposelessness. Questions of culture had been relegated to the bottom of the agenda and all other questions seemed to have precedence. But it is our profound conviction that questions of culture are precisely the primary ones, that this, amidst questions of the spiritual education of the personality, is in fact where discussion should begin.

Applied to architecture and urbanism, we see that the path towards originality and identity lies in the investigation of land-use. The individual building can only have genuinely 'national' characteristics as part of the broad planning context. What we have now is usually the opposite: a superficial use of ornamentation on facades using carpets and fancy screens. In the amorphousness of the larger urban environment, the 'national' house is reduced to nothing more than fashion or witty tricks.

In its way the dwelling is very properly a storehouse of ethno-cultural traditions. Its reflection of the living structure of family, neighbour and race is perhaps the most stabilising and properly 'conservative' expression of everyday cultural constants. All this does not mean however that the forms of the dwelling are givens fixed once for all time. They are natural, changing, dynamic, and only the autocratic concept of history treats them with dictatorial caprice.

Concrete and Turkmenian polychrome

Vladimir Ataev (*Turkmenia*)

For today's architecture in Turkmenistan, as in other republics, industrialised methods of construction are very characteristic. 90 percent of the state housing construction in our republic is based on such methods, and monolithic systems are being developed up to 12 and 16 storeys. At the same time numerous public buildings, using a rich variety of constructional techniques, have been widely praised amongst the professional community.

From the most ancient times the peoples inhabiting Turkmenia demonstrated a building culture of high sophistication in their places, temples and dwellings, as well as decorative and applied arts. Our historical architecture is world-famous in particular for such 10th- and 12th-century masterpieces as

the Mausolea of Sultan Sandzhara in ancient Merv and of Tiurabek-Khanym in Kunia-Urenche. Today there is increasing conviction in the necessity for preserving any of those design features which were used so conspicuously well by Turkmen people in the past and remain relevant today.

The features which were carried forward over the centuries as traditional were the characteristic Turkmenian polychrome, the laconic form and simple applied decoration, the use of light and shadow effects, and the capacity to create very long-lasting and harmonious structures from local handicraft materials. Equally important as a source of inspiration today was the masterly ability of the nomadic Turkmen tribes to create pleasant living environments in the complex natural conditions of the desert.

Unfortunately the historical fate of these peoples has meant that very few of their buildings have survived, and where they have, it is generally in archaeological sites. For the typical town-dweller of today, therefore, the traditional culture is as if it had never been. The few extant examples of their superbly climatically adjusted dwellings are constantly studied now by designers in seach of vernacular inspiration for new housing. So far, however, this process is going on only as experimental work within the region's zonal research institute, so any hope of widespread influence on residential developments is at present premature.

Vernacular influence has so far made a bigger impact on the strongly three-dimensional forms of public buildings, in their volumetric planning and surface treatment. This influence is also very noticeable in the way architects of the republic have turned to monolithic reinforced concrete, for its unlimited plastic possibilities in these respects. The State Republican Library, several big hotels, and a new commercial centre are among recent Turkmen building complexes that have been widely praised for skilful volumetric and spatial exploitation of concrete and their spatial relationship to site features.

Thus the best of current Turkmen architecture is good, but certainly the average level is significantly lower, and much work relies on simplified repetition of what the pioneers have used with sophistication elsewhere. The widespread use of exposed concrete, for example, owes too much perhaps to the outstanding success of the Republican Library. Many are rightly censorious of the way that whole towns have been covered in heavy grey concrete, in disregard of Turkmen traditions of colour. Tashkent is often quoted as an example, for the colourful decorativeness of its architecture. On the other hand many of us would argue forcefully against imitation of Tashkent practice here. Mindless application of colour everywhere does not solve any problems. In our tradition, colour was always directly related to the composition and function of the building, to the lighting situation and a mass of other contextual factors. Certainly there is scope for the use of coloured concretes within our architecture, to lighten larger masses. The roof of the recent new commercial centre in Ashkhabad, for example, would have perhaps profited from that device.

Another approach to extending the colour palette which is being investigated lies in refining the techniques of applying ceramic facings to elements of prefabricated construction, and individual splashes of colour emphasis created by integral works of monumental art are another way of reinterpreting features of our historic environmental traditions. Certainly rerooting ourselves into the national colour 'culture' is a difficult process, like everything in this field, which requires long study of its near-forgotten rules.

Moving from the desirable to the actual, we see all too clearly that today's town planning activity operates by aesthetic categories which have very little in common with regional traditions. In the design consciousness here, it is the ideal of the European city, irrelevant as it may be, which still rules strongest. We have unexpressive, undifferentiated housing areas, where the courtyard, the street and the square have been forgotten. Cultural change however complicates the reassessment of these models, for in new developments the people establish almost no links on the basis of neighbourly proximity. Meanwhile in the traditional environment, that sort of community communication was the main school of social values, regulating the moral and behavioural climate within the living space concerned. Whether that pattern will return with the recreation of those spatial features remains to be seen.

The Valikhanov Museum

Making history accessible by means of architecture

Bek Ibraev (*Kazakhstan*)

We often hear it said that national forms are more successfully achieved by a master from another culture, who sees the uniqueness and particular character of an aesthetic environment from the outside. Examples often quoted from Russian architectural history are such men as Fiorovante, Falconet and Rastrelli. But that is to overemphasise specific internal 'differentnesses' in culture, at the expense of the integral system of connectivities by which it really preserves its existence in its own society. A real expression or reinterpretation of these, it seems to me, demands the deeper sensibilities of the indigenous artist.

I agree entirely with my colleague Karimov in his assertion that national traditions can and should be most powerfully manifested in museum and memorial buildings. In creating a museum to our national hero Chokan Valikhanov not far from the republican capital of Alma-Ata, we pursued this philosophy. Our inspiration was the most widespread of the ancient types of mausoleum, called the *tort-kulak*, which evolved from the ancient Kazakh habit of stopping before 'the house of the spirit of the dead', and was a building with four corners, connected in Kazakh cosmogony with the four corners of the Universe. In general such 'total symbolism' is characteristic of any popular art, and it was particularly

SEIDALIN, IBAEV, VALIKHANOV MUSEUM, 1980-2

appropriate here, as Valikhanov, the great enlightener of the Kazakh people, devoted a large part of his life to studying precisely these aspects of traditional culture.

The four corners of our museum differ in height according to their significance in the symbolism of the Universe. From each of them beams run into the centre which becomes 'a node of happiness'. In the popular imagination it is precisely in the centre of the world that all its levels are united, and well-being comes from the sky. The seven layers of Earth are represented in the museum's terraced floor, so that the visitor gradually rises, as if to the mountain, on a spiral around the central axis. At the lowest level it connects with the hall in memory of Valikhanov, where memorabilia and his own things are exhibited. At the very highest level, where one can touch the ceiling-sky with the hand, are located the collections of applied art from the Kazakhs, Kirgizians, Uigurs, Dungans and other peoples whom Valikhanov studied.

Colour also has symbolic significance here. The walls have the surface texture of fabrics and are red, for in the traditional aesthetics that is the colour of the walls of a house, of the frame of a yurt, of carpets. This is the colour of our level of the world. The floor is blackish-red, corresponding to the underground world. The ceiling is white: soaring to various heights and not touching the walls, this is the sky. The palette here is characteristic of many aspects of Kazakh applied art: carpets, ribbons, bags. It proved its success when full strip-screens from nomads' traditional circular felt tents, the yurts, were displayed here at full length for the first time ever in a museum. The symbolism of each corner is reinforced by the colours of the tassels hanging in each, black in the northern corner, red in the south, yellow in the east and white in the west – all being traditional associations.

As important to our conception as the form and colour was the lighting. We devised an original system that gave even top light for all positions of the sun and freed walls for display. Here light nowhere dazzles the eyes but creates the feeling that the space is full of air, and the spiral sequence of floor levels creates great peace and calm through its non-intersecting flow of visitors. The showcase were designed by the architects as wooden frames with three panes of glass, through which, as we saw it, walls and hangings would be illuminated without spoiling the overall mood of the interior. Unfortunately the display designers did not manage to make full use of this effect of exhibits floating in air, and the displays are rather traditionally done.

The museum's surroundings are laconic,

even austere. Everything is focused on the interior space and subordinated to it. We are not accustomed to use the word 'temple' in respect of museums, but in practical terms these two concepts are equivalent. For the educative and enlightening tasks are not only solved by posters and displays. Of far greater importance is often the person's spiritual state after their visit or in their moment of entering the memorial space.

I think that the symbolism incorporated into the museum will be equally readable to the people of the future, judging by the way that books on history, ethnography and archaeology are instantly snapped up by the mass population these days. People want to know about their own culture, the life and history of their own people. And this interest shows no signs of weakening. On the other hand, the museum is enjoyed most of all by visitors of the older generation. To them it is even more comprehensible. All the signs live on in the people, the visitors explain the colour symbolism, the materials and the details to each other, to the children. Certainly only artists, historians and the old understand the finer details, but the tasks which we set ourselves have seemed in general to be widely comprehensible.

Siberia: land of the future

Alexander Rochegov (*Moscow*)

Geographically, Siberia is vast. Its physical extent and its geological and biological diversity are commensurate. Even its southernmost strip has an extraordinarily rigorous climate.

Culturally the main effect of these factors has been the development of a very special character in its people, typified as highly masculine and stoic, wilful and determined. The area is also characterised by a particular pattern of settlement reflecting the dynamism of that process of territorial conquest of the Siberian wastes which has been the basis of life here. As we approach the 21st century the rhythm of this dynamic is increasing sharply, with dramatic impact on both the relatively old and established centres as well as the newly founded ones.

The areas of Siberia now being developed are creating severe difficulties in respect of human working conditions. Very typical is the large-scale development going on in the West Siberian territorial and productive complex. The 'capital' of the largest oil and gas region here is Tiumen, a town founded in 1586. As the centre of a 'district' embracing 1,435,000 square kilometres with a rapidly rising population, Tiumen has been the originator of a new, so-called 'expeditionary' approach to organising the working and living environment, to replace the usual concept of stable, long-term 'towns' with temporary 'base-camps' for working periods. The problem of tradition and the aesthetic character of buildings in Siberia as a whole is particularly great, as there is no continuity between the present population and any previous inhabitants, nomadic or settled, and there is also a particularly acute disproportion between the volume and speed of construction required and the paucity of qualified architects in these regions.

II: THE CITY AND HISTORY

What will Moscow be like?

Inserting the old in the new: on one of the major problems of Moscow

Alexei Gutnov (*Moscow*)

In discussing questions of the proper relationship of old and new building in the city, the term I like to use is 'concealed reconstruction'. By that I mean that buildings have the right to enter into the historically developed environment only to the extent that they take account of the very complex circumstances of their historical and architectural context. In the old districts of our cities we should use everything that is usable. Where it is genuinely impossible to preserve and reuse the stock, the new must enter the old in such a manner as to become a part of it, to 'conceal itself'. This requires a very particular design approach, which has so

GUTNOV ET AL, STOLESHNIKOV ALLEY PROJECT, 1982-3

far not been acquired by all Moscow architects. We must rapidly reconstruct our approach to make the method of concealed reconstruction a central part of our armoury.

But the profundity of the problem is not in the architect's work alone, for sure. Suppose we have a talented architect's solution to a problem on the drawing board, how are we to build it? The fact is that at present we do not have the resources or skills or the hardware in the building industry that are necessary to start widespread reconstruction work in the city centre. We must create these resources by the very fastest means available to us. Even a one-year delay here can become a five-to-ten year delay in achieving all our further plans.

Just now we are starting a serious and important chunk of work on the new General Development Plan for Moscow, which is to determine our actions up to the year 2010. This means that we are already taking it upon ourselves to make statements about the 21st

century, and must fully understand the responsibility imposed on us in this connection. What is most important here? The main thing, in my view, consists in the simple but all the same paradoxical idea of comprehending the real physical dimensions of the city. The effect of our uniform five-kopek metro fare is to make us all inwardly feel we live in the city centre, and that everything outside the centre is a sort of 'makeweight'. In actual fact the historically developed central part comprises today less than five percent of the territory of the city, and for all its treasures it cannot be allowed to determine the entire face of the capital, though we well understand its role.

Sometimes in lecturing to students I pose the question: what proportion of the city's territory does the centre occupy? And as a rule I hear the answer 20, 30, maybe 40 percent. That shows how inclined we are to exaggerate the size of this territory in our minds, which in itself is a reflection of its high importance. But looking objectively we see that what stretches before us is a gigantic formation which long ago exceeded the conceptual dimensions of a single compact city. Probably it is necessary to work out a separate policy for each of its various different zones, for Moscow today is a city of many towns. And each of them, like the centre, requires its own planning policy, specifically calculated to its needs.

I shall concentrate on what to me seems the most important thing: that somehow we must try to turn back in, upon the city itself, that colossal inner energy which is bursting it open and forcing it to spread outwards onto ever newer and newer sites. Because if we allow the city to expand any further we shall not be able to put the inside of it in proper order. This idea seems to me extremely important to the social, economic and physical development of Moscow.

This is not only a question of the use of very valuable urban land. When we are constantly building on new territory we are eroding the urban infrastructure; we condemn ourselves to the necessity of constructing many kilometres more of high-capacity utilities and transportation systems, first of all the metro. Thus we are building up obligations and burdens of this kind for the whole city. Further development outwards will bring good to no-one. For what does such expansive development mean? It is chronic shortmeasure, chronic shortchanging for the rest of time, for all who remain in the established parts of the city.

What is happening today in the middle areas of the city? We are talking here of what once were Moscow's industrial outskirts, and in practical terms this zone is in a worse position than the centre, or than the periphery where we have built the new districts. Is this not paradoxical, that the working-class heart of Moscow, capital of the world's first proletarian state, should be in this condition? It means that we must rapidly get on with the integrated reconstruction of this whole zone. Intergrated reconstruction – this is not just putting the industrial units themselves into

first-rate order: it is the reconstruction of whole areas of housing and all the elements of the social infrastructure which are located in them. Nor, by the way, does this prevent us from thinking about how we could directly involve the businesses located here in the work of servicing the city. At a time like now, this is the kind of line we should be taking with these businesses: 'Dear friends, since you happen to be located in the centre of Moscow, would you please be so good as to pay for the place that you occupy. And pay the full sum please: stop expecting roads, communications and so on to be given to you as gifts from the city.'

That sort of strategy would mean a lot of work, but it could lead in the end to very interesting results, for it is precisely this part of the city which can give us symbols and images of the 21st century. And at the same time it is all outside the true historical core. Let's build our really modern projects here, as a showplace for what we are capable of as we approach the new century.

If we go even further from the centre, into the outlying districts which have appeared in the last 15 or 20 years, here they have their own problems. They are all very different, and each needs its own distinctive approach. Take the districts of five-storeyed building, for example. Plainly it is absurd to wait for the moment when we have to demolish all that five-storeyed stock and replace it with new. It is time to begin gradually reconstructing these areas. A large part of the stock is technically first class and must undoubtedly be preserved. Besides, we are not only talking of five-storeyed buildings here. Within these areas there are some 9-, 12-, 16-, and even 22-storeyed housing blocks. It is important to bring a more human look to the living environment itself and again to direct attention towards courtyards, the local streets, clearly

ROCHEGOV ET AL, VORONTSEVO HOUSING, MOSCOW

organised internal living environments. What can be done in this direction? In particular, we must increase the density of development in many districts by low- and medium-rise housing, by changing our attitude to the stereotype associated with this kind of building.

If we look at the peripheral areas of Moscow on the understanding that we operate not only with 16-storeyed buildings, but also with this low- and medium-rise construction, we shall find very many sites which we can develop within the present planning structure of these areas, to the great benefit of the entire city.

I venture to suggest that we could build within the Moscow ring-road something of the order of 10 to 15 million square metres more housing than is currently planned, if we radically changed our attitude to the constructional basis of our work. We seem now to be entirely in the power of builders; they have us on a leading rein. This situation has to be broken. At the moment serious reconstruction of our whole system of capital construction is under way. And we Moscow architects must not simply tag along behind events in this process. We must lead the way.

It is difficult to dispute the builders' claims that they can build housing more easily and more cheaply if they do it in vast complexes rather than by selective programmes that combine new building with renovation and reconstruction. But the time requires architects, designers, all workers in the construction industry, and finally the planning organisations – Moscow City Planning office in particular – to assess the situation realistically, to work together on creating a programme of genuine social, economic and physical development for the city. Only by uniting our energies can we solve that problem in a fully responsible way.

Approaches to using the vernacular in Tashkent and Navoi

Tulkinoi Kadyrova (*Uzbekistan*)

In Tashkent today, the most conspicuous example of an innovative approach to assimilation of the architectural heritage is the 16-storeyed housing structure on the corner of Lenin Street and Cosmonauts Prospect by a team under O P Aidinova. This experimental building is our first constructed with sliding shuttering, but its new spatial feature is the internal courtyards created at upper levels for recreation and children's play. In this and other respects ideas we see it as a reference point for future housing design. In the microdistricts of Chirchik, Samarkand and Angren, experiments are under way in using the ancient concept of the *makhallia*, whose prototypes still function successfully in the old-town areas of Tashkent, Samarkand and Bukhara, as a social basis for the structure of new residential areas.

Central Tashkent, as rebuilt since the earthquake, was one of our first attempts to draw upon vernacular traditions, but it has also been amongst the most misunderstood by outsiders. To keep structures clear of the fault-line, the scale of the centre was vast: 1,5000 thousand hectares, and a main axis five kilo-

metres long, which seemed to exclude all possibilities for historical reference. The solution chosen was symbolic: the core of the city would be an oasis, where individual buildings were spread amidst vast areas of green. Shade-giving trees grow slowly, and not all the planned buildings are built, even now, but the concept was powerful for local people and as a design influence thereafter. It was certainly a very different scale and approach from the decorative stylisation more recently used for creating historical reference points in the new Tashkent Metro, where the best stations of the first line, such as Pushkin, Khamid Alimdzhan and Lenin Square incorporated features characteristic of the old palace and civic architecture of our region.

Even larger, though, was the task of creating an entire new city at Navoi. Here the concept was again related to the oasis, featuring luxuriant greenery, a multitude of canals, fountains and children's pools as well as particular attention to detail and finishes in public

HOUSING, TASHKENT, 1970s

spaces. The basic colour scheme of the whole development was set by the white facing tiles of the multi-storeyed brick buildings and white marble chips in the wall panels of others, with more active colours in balconies and galleries, in particular the sky-blue and green hues traditional to vernacular and historical architecture throughout Central Asia.

The future begins yesterday and develops tomorrow

The reconstruction of old Tbilisi

Nodar Mgaloblishvili (*Georgia*)

Much of the paradox and complexity of architecture derives from the fact that on one hand it lags behind the age somewhat – for we are always living in the designs of yesterday – but on the other hand it outstrips its own time, always creating the structures in which we shall live tomorrow. In the face of monotonous uniformity of yesterday our people started looking to the past before most others in the Soviet Union, and the beautifully composed ensembles and individual buildings of Georgia's historically evolved towns began to sparkle with a special light. One result was a spontaneous wave of 'retro' style; deeper and more satisfactory was their new-found concern with the old itself.

Throughout the Soviet Union are historic towns of unique form and appearance. In each of them the rebirth of old districts for contemporary uses is taking place in a different way, using tactics specifically designed for each

case. In their first work on the capital, Tbilisi, Georgian architects recognise certain mistakes, but by now they have some confidence in applying their approach and experience.

The structure of Tbilisi is complex. It runs over 40 kilometres in the narrow gorge of the river Kura. The tightest points contain the ancient districts like the city centre itself, with patterns of building that are highly picturesque and entirely unique to Tbilisi, but are now extremely dilapidated. Through this medieval structure, however, with all its later overlays, run several of the modern city's main arteries, committed to heavy loading by the integrated transport scheme which is already incorporated into the city's approved long-term plan. The task is therefore complex and delicate.

One of the first projects tackled was the reconstruction of Baratashvili Street, a strong transverse highway whose new two-level road bridge connects left and right banks of this highly linear city.

One side of the street is built up with modern buildings, the other had low-value mainly single-storeyed development whose demolition revealed unknown remains of the ancient fortress walls. The initial project for this district proposed eight-to-twelve-storeyed housing here, but already in the 1960s the city's architectural community was protesting at such invasion of the old fabric. After many stages the new project, now completed, has restored both the remaining sections of wall and the traditional housing area with its unique Tbilisi balconies that is adjacent to it.

Reconstruction of this street represented the triumph of ideas that were cherished and preached for years not only by architects, but by writers and artists, historians and art historians in Georgia, who dreamed of restoring this ancient city to its old exoticism. At the same time, problems of creating a new compositional and transport axis for the whole city had to be tackled by the professionals. And there was the higher task, of showing in concrete form what a restored old city for the 21st century might be like.

BATIASHVILI ET AL, OLD TBILISI REBUILDING, 1980s

Success has exceeded all expectations, and it was unanimously decided to apply the same methods to a reconstruction of the whole of the old city. At the same time the designers of new developments, in the outskirts as well as the old districts, have been forced to re-evaluate the questions of human scale, life-style, climate and national mood in their work too. This is an almost equally important result that no-one had dared to anticipate.

On the problems of developing the centre of Kishinev

Iuri Tumanian (*Moldavia*)

The broad professional and public discussions of the Kishinev city centre planning proposals which took place during last year, 1986, revealed basic shortcomings in the practice of developing the central district and in the design solutions proposed for it. During recent decades intensive development of the city centre has included numerous large new buildings as well as greatly improved environmental standards in many public spaces. But the development has been done unsystematically, with no attempt to weave individual objects together into a larger urban composition.

On the city's main route, Lenin Prospect, high dominant elements erected on the perimeter have destroyed any sense of an organic logic in the city structure. Elsewhere both location and architecture of the new Palace of Pioneers have little connection with the street pattern or the building's own function. In another major development the new central

SOLOMINOV ET AL, PEACE PROSPECT, KISHINEV, 1980s

department store and the high bulk of the Communications Ministry create a space that is too broad to be a Prospect and has lost the definition to be a street. Small 19th-century buildings of considerable architectural merit have lost all connection with their surroundings and been condemned to stagnation.

In the process of city-wide discussion some very extreme views were expressed, in favour of blanket preservation of the entire centre in what is effectively its late 19th-century state. When much of the fabric is so morally and technically obsolete as to be causing acute social problems, the people are justifiably demanding their environmental rights. It is not our task to make time stand still out of love for the past.

If we are to preserve a building as an architectural monument then we must be professionally certain that it has genuine aesthetic value independent of fashionable pressures. An integrated reconstruction of the city requires equally serious reconstructions of attitude from all participants in the city's development process, from the municipal leadership to the builder of a small individual house, and plenty of obstacles lie on that path.

The new is not found on the surface, but has to be battled for through the processes of experimentation which must accompany the openness we call *glasnost*. Right now we are awaiting the results of a nationwide competition for the centre of Kishinev, and are hoping it will provide the stimulus for a qualitative leap in our whole handling of the city, as well as revealing the best solutions and the best talents for the centre.

Riga & the small towns of Latvia

History, planning problems and contemporary life

Ianis Drippe (*Latvia*)

Looking at the state of architectural and planning affairs in our capital city, Riga, the Latvian architect ought perhaps to feel satisfied. But is he, as an inhabitant of the city? The answer is No, for larger forces are shaping the relationship between Riga and the rest of the country in a way he sees as counterproductive.

Thanks to the unusual foresight and continuity of planning leadership, the post-war period in Riga saw a series of three General Plans taking the city up to the year 2000, which already provided a very open planning structure based on sophisticated consideration of natural factors and the legacy of historic architecture. The early 1980s have seen the finalising of a detailed project for the famous medieval city centre, whose quality, along with the city's overall economic importance, has made it the effective regional capital of the whole Soviet Baltic area. The plan makes highly imaginative use of the River Daugava with its loops and islands, of the canal around the old fortifications, and of the capitalist town inside the railway ring, with its unique perimeter development from before 1914. This centre contains monuments of National Romanticism, Jugendstil, Eclecticism, and Verticalism as well as the Functionalism of the 1920s and 1930s, and the approach to communications and pedestrian movement has enabled all this historical material to be preserved in a dynamic, far from 'museum-like' spirit. Wherein then lies the concern?

It lies in the fact that despite proposals for controlling the Riga agglomeration, there has been far too large a polarisation in the distribution of cultural and social potential, and of industrial and human resources, between the city and the rest of the Republic. At 900,000 people, Riga is twice the size of Tallin and Vilnius, which are its nearest Baltic competitors, and three times the size of Kaunas. It contains 37 percent of Latvia's total population, and 54 percent of all who work in industry. This situation is a gross distortion of the whole pattern of settlement, and hence culture, within the Baltic states. Now, as historically, this pattern is characterised by the very large numbers of small- and medium-sized towns of 10,000 to 100,000 people, and by the importance of the villages and the farmstead complexes of the agricultural countryside.

When Latvia's 'second-level' towns are Daugavpils and Liepaia, at 120,000 and 110,000, and then Iurmala and Elgava at 60,000 and 57,000, the problem is not just

distortion of the smooth hierarchy by hypertrophy of its peak. It is that precisely these smaller towns are by universal consent the optimal places for the living, working, cultural and creative activities of human beings. They are compact and individual, having developed over long histories.

We have no new towns in the Baltic area; the whole direction followed by Latvia, like the rest, has been based on the wisdom of developing these networks of small towns, restructuring each according to its needs. The very lack of overall population growth that made this possible is now what makes the exaggerated growth of Riga so threatening. We had a process that was proceeding peacefully, and we need to get back to some long-term advance thinking about it.

ALKENIS ET AL, IURMALA SANATORIUM, RIGA, 1978-82

History and landscape: nature and the living environment of Minsk

The Belorussian school of landscape architecture

Eugeny Kovalevsky (*Belorussia*)

Andrei Burov, one of the founder-figures of Soviet architecture, wrote that 'it would be logical not just to build leisure resorts for recovering from the absurdities of the city, but so to build cities themselves that there is no need to recover from them.' This is a challenge which subsequent Soviet town planners have taken seriously, as is manifested by the extensive open spaces and water-greenery systems they have created in cities as far apart as Moscow and Erevan, Kiev and Tbilisi, Kaliningrad and Omsk, Donetsk and Sochi, and with conspicuous success in the new housing districts of the Baltic states.

Belorussia is interesting in this respect, because it has built on a long-established tradition of organic interaction between architecture and nature, exemplified in such towns as Vitebsk, Mogilev, Gomel, Brest, Grodno, Mozyr, Lida, and many others, to develop what may be called a Belorussian school of urban landscaping. Its main feature is the use of water-greenery systems as a generative and structural influence on the city itself, and builds upon the fact that Belorussian towns are very commonly located along relatively slow-flowing, open rivers.

The republican capital of Minsk suffered massive destruction in the last war, involving the loss of parks and surrounding woodlands as well as the built fabric. Its river, the Svisloch, has always been a poor irrigation source, due to the hydrographic characteristics of the Minsk Hills where it rises. Green spaces were a key element of the post-war reconstruction project, but by the late '60s economic growth had produced a water crisis which was solved through the massive Vileisko-Minsk water project of 1970-76, which increased the width of the Svisloch in its bed by some five times, to reach 600 metres in places.

Seven stepped cascades constructed as its regulation system became the axis of a bold diameter of water and greenery to form the main compositional axis in the city plan, comprising an unbroken system of city and district parks, gardens, boulevards, squares and green embankment areas which penetrate the whole fabric of the city. Further out, extending over 50 kilometres, flood pools and small tributaries of the Svisloch form a water-park ring of similar diversity which so transforms the environmental character of the new housing districts that its fundamental function for industry is forgotten by most of the population as

ZHLOBO ET AL, GREEN MEADOW, MINSK, 1980s

they enjoy the city's 50 square kilometres of recreational reservoirs and 36 kilometres of artificially created beaches. Minsk's Development Plan promises that by the year 2000 water and greenery will comprise 50 percent of the city's total area. The underlying concept has roots in the historical traditions of the Belorussian people, but we like to think that what we are doing now involves the creation of a tradition of our own time as well.

The regional approach
Returning to old sources

Ado Eige (*Estonia*)

The ideas I shall discuss here are born of the situation in the Estonian Republic and in that sense are themselves regional. They make no pretence to represent any general tendency within the Soviet Union, though they derive from the widespread concern to respond to change without erasing the historical codes from our nation's collective memory.

The criteria for judging architecture naturally change over time, as the cultural level and economic possibilities change, and with them cultural contacts, fashion and the so-called 'spirit of the times'. For example, by looking at Post-Modernism as a method and mode of thinking, the theories of Venturi allow us to approach some of our most difficult tasks with better understanding. They allow us to see architecture today not only in the light of technical and material possibilities, but with the perceptions of that public opinion through which architecture has to be brought to the stage of being built. Amidst all the absurdities, they permit us to create an architectural thinking which can use all those conflicts, compromises, confusions and deviations from the norm which otherwise seem obstructions to our task, and with the help of irony to give a building various meanings, a covert and an overt symbolism. In a word they enable us to create an architecture that positively embraces the real factors operating on it through society and the politics of the building process. We arrive thereby at what one may call a regional Post-Modernism: an architecture genuinely born of the local convictions.

The optimism of early Functionalism and the post-war attraction to massive urban renewal caused much of the destruction we now regret. Much of this monotony and inhuman scale that resulted derived from the fact that Modernism regarded the city as a once-and-for-all completed quantity, in which the focus of architectural aspirations was the individual building.

Our new conviction of the need to preserve and reuse both old buildings and entire old districts represents a recognition of the importance of this most visible part of the social capital on which today's culture has grown. The result is more rational analysis of the urban environment. We see the town as something changing over time, not as the finished urban model conceived by Modernism. Philosophically as well as formally, therefore, it is a return to the heritage, and this is the basis on which we are trying to handle the future of Tallin.

Low-rise development: what is in favour?
Experience in Kaunas

Gezhiminis Girchis (*Lithuania*)

In the Soviet Union, low-rise building normally means scattered, freestanding cottages on the traditional rural model. Such housing can certainly enrich large-scale, high-rise developments by introducing variety, but my subject here is low-rise building of a type that fully satisfies the diverse requirements of today's city dweller. That is low-rise at high density.

Though well understood abroad this concept has only recently started to get attention here. Some developments have been completed, notably in Kaunas and Shauliia, as a result of studies by this republic's Institute for the Design of Urban Construction and its Kaunas branch. Professionals involved are convinced it has a serious future, and surveys of inhabitants are very positive. But we need to be quite clear as to what its specific advantages are, and how and where to use it.

The type which has proved most applicable to our problems is the two-storeyed terraced house with semi-basement. Its form allows combinations of house size, from three to five habitable rooms, within a group. Any individual unit can be expanded as family requirements change, by extending the ground floor, equipping the roofspace or semi-basement for occupancy. Private motorcars can be accommodated economically, as well as conveniently, in the semi-basement. At the same time each dwelling can be allocated a small plot of land for inhabitants to design as they choose, which contrasts sharply with the anonymous open space of the high-rise developments. The

OLD CITY RESTORATION AREA, VILNIUS

24-dwelling complex recently completed in Kaunas shows the great effectiveness and economy of such a solution.

What of the public advantages? Most importantly, such building enables us to develop urban land which is unsuitable for high-rise because of its relief, its bearing capacity, the expense of servicing it, or the presence of old buildings. Analysis of unused land in Vilnius showed that about 4,000 units of terraced housing could be located in the area concerned without prejudice to the high-rise already there. Low-rise in this context supplements and adds aesthetic diversity. A project for the vast Shiliania housing area of Kaunas demonstrated this well, and we all know that every city has land in these categories.

Almost equally valuable is the way that building of this scale and type can harness resources and effort from industrial enterprises, trades unions, and the direct participation of future inhabitants themselves, into the housing process. And if we turn to the currently very topical subject of housing the young, the advantages of low-rise terraced housing for that sector are unarguable.

Low-rise, high-density is not something to replace our existing approach, but to supplement it, and we need to start looking urgently at the organisational options for exploiting its many qualities.

MODERNISM AS TRADITION

Iuri Volchok

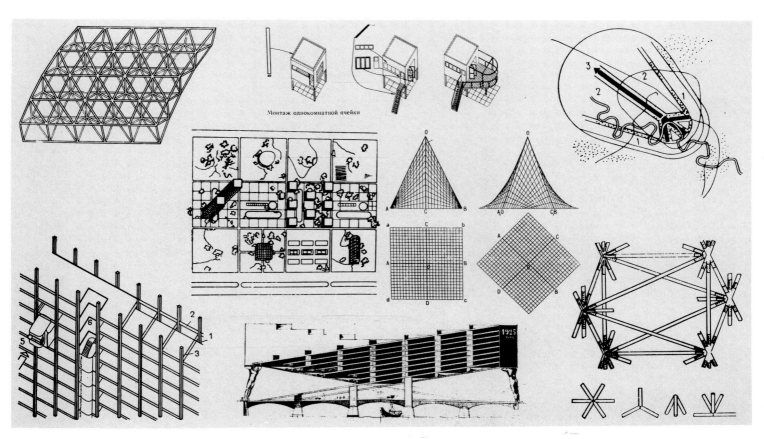

Монтаж однокомнатной ячейки

It is one of the particular features of life today that architecture – and with it the architect – is being charged in the name of history with the social balance sheet of its activities. In the Soviet Union the atmosphere of the 70th anniversary of the 1917 Revolution, which is being celebrated this year, has naturally brought its own influence to bear on the content and orientation of those charges.

Examining this in greater detail, one of the key issues is that of the perceived relationship between recent and less recent history. Discussion of architecture between architects and society during the last few years has shown that in the public mind the concept of history exists fairly universally as History with a capital 'H', and is therefore almost automatically orientated towards the distant past. Their assumptions are summed up in a phrase: 'the older, the more historic'. This creates a scale of values, both in relation to the heritage of history and culture, and in the evaluation of the realities of the historically evolved city, which is effectively unquestioned, and, indeed, considered incontestable. At the same time, history has ceased to be the preserve of a marginal section of society. It has become the all-pervading interest of the whole population, and is naturally stimulating demands for the preservation of those remains of earlier material culture which are perceived to embody spiritual values.

I do not argue with that. I want only to assert the professional importance of basing such a policy on an attitude which is equally respectful to all strata of time: to ancient history, the medieval, the modern industrial era and the most recent period. Our accumulated legacy from the past is as important for establishing the time-links which ensure a balanced and coherent environment in the contemporary city, as for the preservation of culture per se. Different eras achieve intellectual and technical mastery of their history in different degrees, but in the art of architecture as we see it today, the ability to establish a relationship with the heritage of all epochs is the essential qualification for working within the historic city.

From the perspective of history itself, 70 years is as nothing, and the whole existence of the Soviet Union slots into the period studied as 'recent history'. That itself has a special importance for the development of culture and society. It is the most recent history which forms the link between the past and the future, and is therefore concerned not so much with yesterday's values as with the definition of values that will be socially important for the future.

The first 70 years of Soviet architecture, therefore, are not just a part of the heritage to which we will address ourselves with whatever our quotient of imagination. They are an organic contribution to the history of culture in our country and to wider

37

IURI VOLCHOK

processes of world development in our own time. This recent architectural history should therefore be among the first objects of our attention when we concern ourselves with links between the past and the future, and hence with preservation. In this area ignorance is unpardonable, and loss is something which can never be culturally replenished.

What were some of the innovations which make the architecture of the 1920s and 1930s such a significant link here? Let us look first at the field of architectural morphology.

The restructuring of social relationships was the central concern of those years, but it was accompanied by the rethinking of many related concepts. 'Construction' was a concept that took on a much broader humanitarian content than previously. It became the metaphor for socially meaningful structures; it became the structural principle inspiring pursuits of 'the new' in the art, literature, theatre and cinematography of those years, and also in architecture.

Ironically here it is the tectonic innovations, those involving the spatial implications of new technology, which have been least studied, though they are most germane to this theme.

The seminal projects conceived by the leaders of the avant-garde are well known. Tatlin's scheme for a monument and headquarters for the Third International, of 1919, had demonstrated the aesthetic possibilities of a new spatial synthesis with a maturity which seemed an embodiment of the whole corpus of the 20th century's new thinking on spatial and tectonic problems. It was a design so pregnant, so open-ended, that it provided inspiration for the whole of the next generation. The Vesnin brothers' projects for the Palace of Labour of 1923 and the Leningradskaia Pravda building of 1924, like Melnikov's designs for a multi-storey garage in Paris of 1925, were integrations of the functional and constructional aspects of organising space. Leonidov's proposals for a socialist approach to settlement planning at Magnitogorsk, in 1930, showed the same principles on an even larger scale, and all achieved fame because they were complete architectural projects.

Innovation in the actual geometry of form and in the spatial potential of modern materials received far less attention. Who knows now that on 30th June 1928 T Makarova was granted a patent for spatial enclosure by the hyperbolic paraboloid? The Russian engineer V Shukhov had previously applied this technique to the creation of open-work tower structures, but Makarova was the first to propose them for roofing. Not till after the Second World War were they 'rediscovered' by such designers as Felix Candela. Who knows that July 1931 saw the first timber membrane structure being erected as a thin-walled arched vault over a glass factory in Nizhny Novgorod? Who now recalls the invention of pre-fabricated membrane structures in reinforced concrete by the Soviet engineers I Liudovsky and B Slezinger in the early 1930s? It was Nervi who got those into the textbooks several decades later.

Research into the methodology of construction itself has received even less attention, though work of astonishing power and prescience was achieved. Take for example the ideas about industrialised housing construction produced by Moisei Ginzburg and other Constructivists on the principle of 'replacing atavistic ideas of "building" by the modern concept of "assembly" '. The example from 1930 shown here relates to one-person living cabins for a leisure satellite of Moscow to be called Green City. Nikolai Ladovsky's Green City project produced perhaps the most important single planning concept of those years – the parabolic growth structure for a metropolis. By the time Doxiadis was singing its praises in the 1950s, everyone had also forgotten the stimulus which Ladovsky's dynamic spatial thinking derived from Soviet astrophysicist A Fridman's discovery of the 'expanding universe'. If Ladovsky's concept for the horizon-

tal dimension of the city is not entirely forgotten, the same cannot be said of his equally prescient 'cake-stand dwellings assembled from prefabricated standard elements' within a fixed framework. Le Corbusier's 'Obus' structure for Algiers, which Ladovsky certainly did not know, was contemporaneous. It was a concept based on the same principle of separating functional structures with differing timescales of moral and physical amortisation, a principle that would be seriously reexamined only by such people as the Archigram group in the 1960s (and maybe our English colleagues would be interested to know of Ladovsky's pioneering work), and by Habraken in Holland, Kikutake and Kurokawa in Japan, Ikonnikov and Pchelnikov in the Soviet Union.

One more example from the mid 1930s: the Kharkov professor A Ginzburg, a relative of Moisei, was the first person to publish a form of construction based on the technological principles and the concept of 'the spatial node' which today have become known worldwide, through Buckminster Fuller's application of them, as the 'geodesic dome'.

I do not quote these examples just for the sake of establishing precedents, though that is important, but to impart an idea of the level of technological sophistication underlying the formal innovations of the '20s and '30s, which is an equally important dimension of tradition that we should be building upon today.

As architecture hangs its head before these charges of social failure, there is another aspect of its tradition and its cultural contribution which we should recall. Not for nothing are specialists in the theory and methodology of both the natural and the social sciences looking ever more intently at architecture as a valuable field for experimentation. They point out repeatedly that generating space-time models is a far more productive exploratory tool for them than any inert accumulations of knowledge from one single discipline. They recognise the conceptual skills of such model-building to be sophisticated and beyond the level of many perfectly competent researchers. Why look to architecture? Because the building of space-time models on a given specification is an everyday professional obligation for the architect, and they respect that particular skill in the organisation of tectonic thinking in space as a source of hope for progress in their own fields.

Such relationships help further the respect for architectural professionalism which will restore it to that central role in the development of spiritual culture which we architects recognise as the condition of healthy development in architecture itself.

While the past stands for a continuity of tradition, culture, professional authority, and patriotic mood, the future represents the search for new methods of spatial thinking, economics, building production and again culture – only its level and time-references are different. The relationship between past and future, tradition and innovation in architecture is amongst the oldest of its professional problems. In different places, at different stages of cultural development, it has quite different levels of interpretation. The interest in cultural and professional traditions is far from limited, however, to questions of how colour and decoration may be applied to the 'body' of the architectural form. The fundamental redefinitions of concepts of 'boundary' in contemporary culture, of the concept of 'wall', have opened the doors onto a new stage of volumetric and spatial ideas about architectural form.

What is architectural form? It is the most value-laden realisation of our tectonic thinking and of our activity with the earth's materials. Those traditions too demand our attention.

Dr Iuri Volchok is Director of the Soviet Architecture Sector of the Institute for the Theory and History of Architecture, Moscow

ENRICHING OUR FANTASY
12 projects by young Moscow architects

Andrei Bokov

SAVVA AND ALEXANDER BRODSKY, ILYA UTKIN, A WALL OF ALEXANDER GREEN'S HOUSE-MUSEUM IN THEODOSIA

This 'exhibition' does not represent a group of like-minded people, or bearers of a single creative concept. Its aim is to show the genuine variety and real potential of our architecture. The commentary is not concerned so much with specific innovations and discoveries (which the reader can find out about himself) as with the more general attitude of the architect to the city and to artistic culture. The urban context and contemporary artistic culture are the main preoccupations of the authors of these 12 designs.

Without a doubt it is the real, surrounding city which has caught the imagination of architects today, pushing aside abstract professional aims, stylistic strivings and aesthetic preferences. The city can be present in one of two ways. Either it is something concrete, say present-day Moscow with its particular space and time, peculiarities and details, types of citizen, urban folklore and toponymy, holidays, workdays and changing seasons (which incidentally alter the face of Moscow more drastically than that of any other European capital). Or it is 'the city as such', representing a certain type of organisation of space and life. 15 to 20 years ago the city was designed and seen as a large house, simplified and homogenous overall. This traditional idea, used in conjunction with a whole new set of techniques, formed the basis for some Soviet designs for 'Cities of the Future' in the 1960s. In the work done today each house is treated as a town (and this idea is not new either), with all its essential features: roads, towers, gates, a centre and periphery, appearing not just as metaphors but also in actual, miniature form.

This approach to the city, or return to it, is accompanied by a typical 'role erosion': the architect eagerly abandons the purely professional sphere that was once so carefully and effectively guarded, and becomes simultaneously an ordinary citizen and a researcher – a 'city specialist' and an artist.

The phrase 'urban environment' represents perhaps the most popular juxtaposition of words in the contemporary professional lexicon. It has informed a varied literature and refers to a specific approach to design – 'the environmental approach'. Within the framework of this approach special attention is now being focused, not on the isolated element or action, but on the borders and transitions, the elements of mediation, relation, union – for example roads, yards, underground passages, boulevards, views, and corners. The building as a unit with a value of its own, as a 'rounded sculpture', is losing its attraction; the status of architecture which is 'good' in isolation is falling, whereas architecture which may be 'bad' in isolation but part of a good, valid environment and an attractive place, such as Arbat or Ulitsa 25 Oktyabrya, increasingly attracts sympathy. The concept of the environment, which arose in the system of ecological consciousness and awareness, is for the architect primarily filled with a figurative content which establishes an elusive integrity over the sum of the buildings.

The spacious and full-blooded shapes of the real city are replacing abstract concepts. In practice this is bringing about a revision and renewal of the whole arsenal of architectural shapes and their construction. The idea of the unity of architecture and man, the citizen and the city, trivial at first sight, acquires a new significance and rouses special interest in what is commonly called 'city life'. The needs and preoccupations of those who will live, walk and feel in the city, have displaced considerations of proportion and composition. The pedestrian's world, the pedestrian street, the pedestrian space as such are considered as a social, cultural value; interest in highways, junctions and cars is considerably reduced among the architects featured here.

The concept of the social centre, the social space, has also noticeably changed, and interest in it has undoubtedly increased. 10 to 15 years ago in the practice of experimental design

1

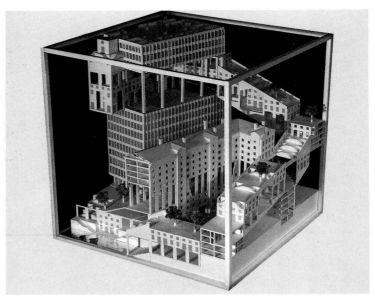

1

and simply in the sphere of interests, it was the theme of the dwelling which prevailed: the dwelling complex, the dwelling unit. And whereas then the centre appeared to the imagination as a separate house or group of houses distributed in emptiness, the centre today is an urban space, a street and a square, interpreted in a somewhat 'renaissance' spirit as interiors roofed by the sky.

Taking the wide spaces between houses, which have been empty in the literal and practical sense as a result of enthusiasm for 'open planning', and making them seem lived in, enriched, filled up; that is one of the rapidly progressing directions taken by design. Within this general movement the 'furnishing of urban spaces' constitutes a particular theme.

The reinterpretation of the intervening, connecting open urban spaces has led to a new look at the suburbs. The suburb becomes in its own way the universal matrix, reproducing and absorbing all the characteristics of the town. The theatre, the school, the monument – any combination of institutions – can successfully be placed around the main, central, collective space whether it be open or enclosed.

Just as any building in the traditional town was both a 'volume'

and an instrument of the urban spatial organisation of square and streets, the contemporary house similarly strives to embody a value beyond its basic function: to serve as gates, a wall, or the foundation to another house. In practice each of the objects shown has 'a double, triple, quadruple value', just like the contemporary citizen who switches from one role to another.

Most of the work shown can be categorised as 'tactical adaptation' taken as 'contextual', with addition, inclusion, the attempt to build in, to base on what already exists or to initiate historical depth and many-layered space undertaken on principle. Reconstruction features not as a genre but rather as a way of thinking directed towards dialogue with one's neighbour, towards cultivation, towards a kind of 'growing' of the town. All this stems not so much from the opportunity of escaping from the problem of seeking and choosing a language and a solution, as from an acknowledgement that only that solution which arises out of the concrete reality and nature of the contemporary town and its environment is valuable.

Those features of the environment which are attractive from the citizen's point of view, but are often inadequate or eroding, become targets and features of design. These include spatial

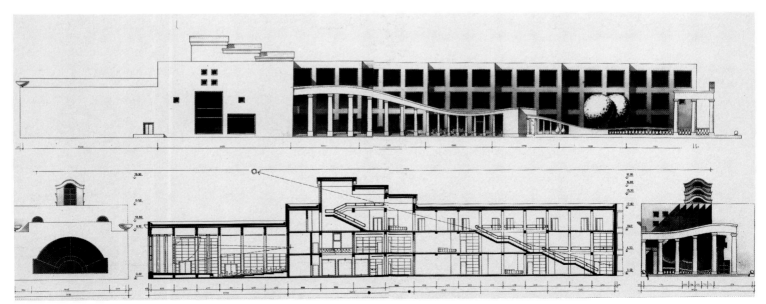

2

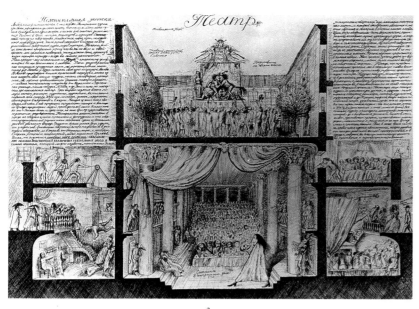

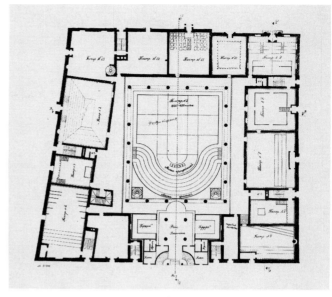

3

3

continuity and multiple layering, variety and multiplicity of scale, the capacity for improvement and for fragmented existence, in a word, using the very popular expression of M Bakhtin, 'polyphony'. It would certainly be difficult to find a more appropriate word to describe the specific Muscovite environment, which is distinguished by the amazing extent to which phenomena, events and characteristics are intertwined.

The architect of today values and feels a party to artistic creativity more than his counterpart did 10 to 15 years ago. Bringing architectural consciousness into the sphere of 'the arts', raising the prestige of the artistic and poetic has meant some drop in interest in rational methods and their application; this has indirectly been reflected in the unpopularity of *thencism* (high-tech). The 'artistic' is clearly conceived not as something additional and non-essential but as part of the inner fabric of the town and of architecture, as the principal means of introducing order and creating an adequate environment.

Architecture is improving and re-establishing its links, which had weakened, with the representational arts. This is not happening so much in terms of a direct link, of a 'synthesis' with painting or sculpture, but rather in the spirit of solving related problems through the art of presentation. The fact that the presence of the 'artistic' in architecture is becoming stronger is reflected by the profusion of designs and competition entries which are experimental and intended not for implementation but for the solution of problems internal to the profession. At any rate most of the work presented here is of that nature. These architects have more right to claim to be independent and to have a creative identity than did their recent predecessors, because they are turning towards the values of urban culture as a whole, including what is local and concrete, everyday, usual, regular. The enthusiasm for Constructivism or for the classical which prevailed in the 1920s and 1950s has been replaced by a more balanced attitude towards our heritage: simultaneously, there has been a rediscovery of the value and integrity of Soviet architecture of the 1930s and 1940s, which, incidentally, is almost unknown in the West.

In conclusion, extensive potential for shape formation was discovered in areas where the architect, in contrast to the poet or artist, had not previously sought it – for example, an old school, a traditional dwelling, or the restricted zone of a railway.

A characteristic of the new shape, which lacks obvious extra-

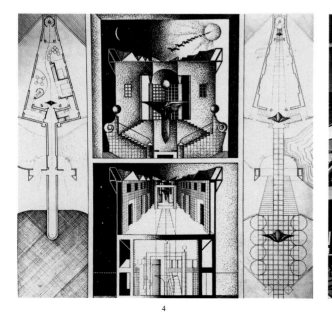

4

5

41

vagance, is that it has meaning, or content. Architecture is reacquiring, or striving to reacquire, its creative role in terms of sense, meaning, and form. The forms of this type of architecture (and it is about such forms that Charles Jencks writes), do not rely solely on association. Their creators do not assume an abstract, exterior, evaluating vision, but instead are involved, inclusive, experiencing architecture in a comparable way to experiencing music, as 'an environmental experience'. Favourite themes of environmental design focus on the theatre, music, or museum – the environment as a whole is theatricized, or museumized, rather than treated merely as the background for a certain type of intervention. A third, no less popular, theme is the 'nursery', where the theme of an environment for achievement, creativity and play is treated, as a rule, seriously and even somewhat ascetically, without any traditional playfulness or features of technical utopianism.

Passing from favourite themes to typical 'means' we note that the sculptural expressiveness of the 1960s preoccupation with abstract form and 'things' has been supplanted by experiments with space, particularly inhabited and domesticated space. The interior space, related to the ouside and fixed in a particular place,

The review of the use of trimmings, presentation, decoration, the rehabilitation of detail and ornament, relies today more than ever on a feeling for the depth and importance of these phenomena, on an understanding of their place and role in human surroundings.

A wall of Alexander Green's house-museum in Theodosia by Savva Brodsky, Alexander Brodsky, Ilya Utkin.
This work may act as a kind of epigraph to the exhibition for, in the opinion of the commentator, it absorbs and reflects many typical features of contemporary awareness within the profession.

1 *The new urban space: a design for the 1980 Sofia World Biennale* by Lev Yevzovich, Andrei Nekrasov, Mikhail Khaysman, Andrei Chel'tsov.
An incidental but typical fragment of urban space, fitting into an imaginary $50m^3$ cube, is reconstructed with the aim of eliminating the negative elements of the environment: excesses or inadequacies of scale, absence of pedestrian spaces and the reduced role of natural contours. The alternative proposed is

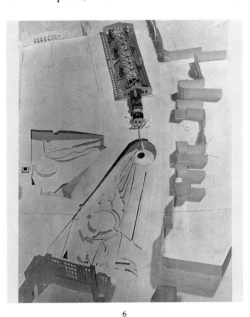

6

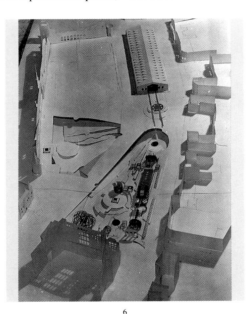

6

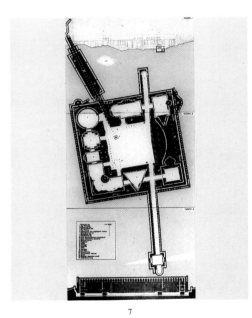

7

orientated and directed – such is the ideal of this architecture.

As before, the sharpest spatial collisions take place within the bounds of the distinction between 'internal-external' or 'interior-urban'. But the conflict is no longer resolved by means of assertion beyond that which take place inside the house, and not even through the interdependence of the outer and inner, but rather in 'mutual convertibility'. With this as the basis for reconstruction, any urban space may be interpreted as internal, as an 'urban interior' to which to apply techniques, means and conceptions which previously were considered unacceptable, whereas within the house urban squares and streets arise.

An interest in the 'meaningful' and 'self-contained' space is the norm in the architecture exhibited, that is in 'Archetypes of the environment', which express first and foremost themselves – the staircase, columns, corner, cornice, door, window, wall, street, bridge, intersection and so on. The combination of these creates a living language of architecture, which is capable of constant development and for which there is no alternative. A return to the archetypes characterised by refined articulation will demonstrate the value of decoration as a means of defining, and revealing, the essential nature of an object.

the new urban space, the 'street-house', made to a human scale, typical urban forms (streets, courtyards, squares) and a new romantic image. The universal, infinite 'street-house' system develops freely above and below the town, permeates existing buildings and allows constant change as required of the density and character of the space's context.

2 *Children's arts school (competition entry)* by Olga Kaverina, Nikolai Kaverin.
The arts school for 150 children consists of three specialised departments – visual, choreographic and musical – which are located on the ground, first and second floors respectively. The school building consists of an elongated three-storey space which, together with the adjacent open courtyard, is defined on the outside by a colonnade of varying modules that turns into a balustrade. The changing size of the columns is explained by the presence of children of every school age, and it reflects the architects' equal respect for every age group. The interior space of the school opens onto the elongated axis towards the auditorium and exhibition hall, so embodying the movement from the creation process to its result, from inability to competence.

3 *'Theatrical Utopia': or ideal conditions for theatrical creation* by Alexander Brodsky, Ilya Utkin, Yelena Markovskaya.
The traditional (but conventional) urban quarter becomes a theatre. Students of various theatrical schools meet in one place: each group, headed by a teacher, is allocated its own room for work, rehearsals and performances, which can be entered directly from the street. The rooms surround a theatrical space, a covered courtyard: during the day this is a place for meeting and social contact; during the evening it is an auditorium with a stage, where the best pieces are performed and discussed.

4 *A detached town house, as an exhibit in a hypothetical museum of 20th-century architecture (design for the Shinkenshiki competition 1981)* by Mikhail Belov, Maxim Kharitonov.
THE VISITOR'S WORLD: coming out of the museum, I found myself in an avenue leading to the House in a Frame. On going up the stairs and entering it, I found myself in an empty street at the end of which stood a house. The street soon finished. The houses became dwarf-like while I turned into a giant. Coming down a staircase I became a midget and found before me a room of enormous proportions – a table towered like a mountain and a

preserved, the street had shed a rich and meaningful layer of ornament, colour and street furniture, a whole set of 'significant' but non-functional items, in particular a section of the Chinatown wall and the gates on its periphery. These are restored, simultaneously making the street 'spatial', three-dimensional, and connecting it with the neighbouring courtyard territories and roofs. Temporary and changing street 'garments' become a means of changing and shaping the form of the street environment.

6 *The theatre on 50th Anniversary of October Square (Manège) in Moscow (competition project for the 'Theatre of the Future')* by Vadim Gudkov, Alexander Lokter, Tatiyana Mashkova, Yerveny Monakhov, Mark Fedorov.
In the centre of Moscow, next to the Kremlin, a new cultural and information centre is created: a square, an area for promenading, fairs, theatrical performances, exhibitions and processions. The environment is transformed with the help of a mobile creation – a huge toy, a 'wonder-horse' – which intermittently rests in the building which used to house the Manège, and comes out into the square.

8

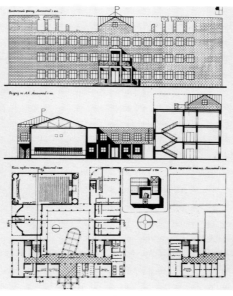

8

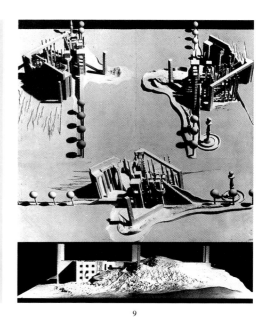

9

bed loomed monstrously. I wandered among huge children's toys and bricks. I saw this same house hanging in the etchings on the wall, and gleaming in the chimney recess. I rushed towards it, but found myself in a long corridor which slanted upwards at the end. My journey was over. I was back where it had all begun, standing in front of the House in a Frame, in which I had been and yet had not been.
THE OWNER'S WORLD: the house we live in is a little strange but it nevertheless has many cosy nooks. Upstairs, on the roof, there is a small cinema where our whole family and our friends watch films. In the rooms we rest after work, and on the mezzanine there is even a small studio where each person enjoys his favourite pastime. We have a large sitting room with a door to the garden. Fruit trees surround the house and there is also a pond in which we bathe. We are very fond of the house we live in.

5 *Improving 25th October Street (a design submitted by 13 students and young architects)* Coordinator: Mikhail Khazanov.
One of Moscow's oldest streets, and today its liveliest pedestrian area, becomes 'the visual experience street', 'the festival street'. Although almost all the surrounding constructions had been

7 *Water theatre on the former estate of Kuskovo near Moscow (competition project for the 'Theatre of the Future')* by Andrei Bokov, Yergeny Budin, Vyacheslav Petrenko, Yury Telitsyn, Andrei Feyst.
The proposed combination of varied but archetypal spaces provides unlimited possibilities for utilisation. The customary hard floor is replaced by a surface of water over which move floats with scenery or floats for spectators and visitors. The water also creates an environment which gives rise to many associations from Roman naumachies and Venetian carnivals to Petersburg fairs and Kuskovo aquatic celebrations.

8 *Conversion of a typical old school into a children's art school (competition project)* by Yury Avvakumov, Alexei Ramensky, Sergei Uspensky.
The building used is a secondary school of the type built in all big cities between 1938 and 1940. The design was by K Jus. Its radical reorganisation is the result of changes in the education process which are leading to the acquisition of these schools for use by administrative institutions.
The architects consider it important to retain the original form

10

10

of the school and use it for new purposes. Possibly this is merely due to nostalgia for their childhood, as they spent it in precisely such schools. They would like to make the detached building part of the urban environment and so have developed it, creating a small courtyard with an arcade encircling its perimeter. A courtyard, forming something of a separate place for games and meetings, is essential for children. By analogy with children's bricks, a collection of functional blocks and a linking arcade was conceived, to be assembled in various combinations.

9 *Memorial to the events and heroes of the Second World War in Dagestan and a space for children's games and education (proposals)* by Vladislav Kirpichev.
These are sculptures which are experienced from inside like towns in miniature. The lines points, surfaces, the geometric figures and bodies, form a space which has significant content. Both works are 'spatial dramas' based on the conflict between the real and the fantastic, between that which is being created and that which is being destroyed, between the integral and the fragmentary, the free and the rational, the predictable and the accidental.

10 *School of Arts (competition design)* by Alexander Boldin, Svetlana Georgieva, Yelena Mitenko, Georgi Muryshkin.
The design unites in a single whole an arts school and a typical dwelling block 18 to 22 storeys high, with provision being made for converting the top storeys of the dwelling area into school premises in the next few years if the need arises. This unusual solution was a result of the following analysis of the state of affairs in contemporary Soviet architecture and traditional Russian architecture.

At present the appearance of a town is shaped by housing, that is by the most popular and typical elements of the environment. This results in a levelling and depersonalisation of the skyline which makes orientation and identification more difficult. The consequences of the non-aesthetic nature of the architectural environment are particularly negative in the sphere of aesthetic education. At the same time it is within the Russian tradition to give weight to social buildings. Traditionally, the concepts of 'exaltation' and 'elevation' coincide to provide a rich artistic and semantic basis for architecture (for example the many-domed Russian churches). A further traditional principle is the use of contrast as a means of achieving richness of

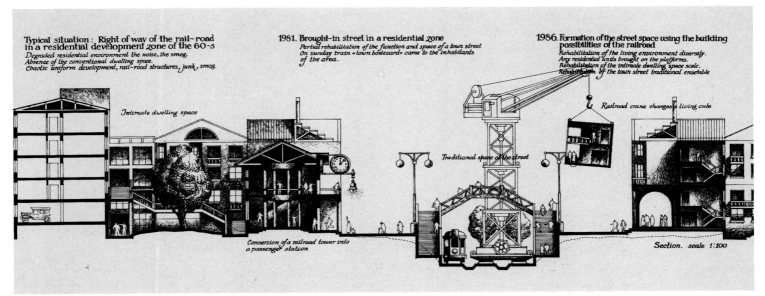

Typical situation : Right of way of the rail-road in a residential development zone of the 60-s
Degraded residential environment the noise, the smog.
Absence of the conventional dwelling space.
Chaotic uniform development, rail-road structures, junk, smog.

1981. Brought-in street in a residential zone
Partial rehabilitation of the function and space of a town street
On sunday train «town boulevard» came to the inhabitants of the area.

1986. Formation of the street space using the building possibilities of the railroad
Rehabilitation of the living environment diversity.
Any residential units brought on the platforms.
Rehabilitation of the intimate dwelling space scale.
Rehabilitation of the town street traditional ensemble

Intimate dwelling space

Traditional space of the street

Railroad crane changes a living cube

Conversion of a railroad tower into a passenger station

Section. scale 1:100

11

11

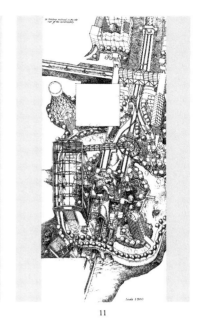

11   11

composition, including situating buildings of varied profile on a massive static base (the lower floor of a wooden house).

The principal aims of the design are to restore the traditional determining role of social buildings within the town plan, and to create individual units immediately within the body of the built-up living area, thus facilitating orientation within housing complexes. The direct combination of the functions of an arts school with a dwelling is an architectural expression of the idea that aesthetic education and daily life are inseparable.

11 *The rehabilitation of the area of the railway encircling Moscow (a design for the UNESCO 'Rehabilitation of a decayed urban environment' competition) by Victor Varlamov, Lev Yerzovich, Andrei Nekrasov, Mark Khaysman.*
This design sets out principles for the adaptation of the most characteristic elements of a railway zone, and entails the conversion of a transport centre where the railway crosses an avenue built in the 1950s into a social centre reminiscent of a traditional pedestrian square. The part of railway territory used for warehouses and a five-storey building built in the 1960s are converted into a traditional urban street. The railway's industrial enter-

prise area becomes a city park, etc. Each endeavour of adaptation is effected in three stages. On the first level the main means of rehabilitation is mobile, travelling architecture: the train-street, the train-boulevard, the train-canal, etc; on the second level the building of stationary constructs including the railroad starts; in the final stage a new, third Moscow ring (the other two being the Boulevard ring and Garden ring) is created, a ring of traditional urban ensembles and mobile architecture.

12 *The 'Sayany' Cinema in Ivanovskoye, a new suburb of Moscow (executed design) by Victor Lebedev, Nikolai Kaverin, Alexander Tsiv'yan, Boris Shabussin.*
The cinema, with two auditoria seating 500 and 300 people, is one of the main components in a community centre currently at the development stage. The whole centre, with internal, partially covered pedestrian passages, is markedly urban in character, contrasting with the spacious and free design of the housing sites. The aim is to create a centre of attraction as rich as possible in urban activity for the population of this peripheral area of Moscow. The cinema itself is resolved as the supremely urban space, simultaneously a crossroads and a gateway.

12

12

PURSUIT OF CONTINUITY

Alexander Kudriavtsev & Alexander Krivov

KUDRIAVTSEV & KRIVOV

THEMES OF CONTINUITY: A PICTORIAL ANALYSIS

Conception by Ilya Lezheva & Andrei Nekrasov
Commentaries by Vyachislav Glazychev & Natalia Dushkina

With this issue of *Architectural Design* and the exhibition in Britain to coincide with it, our aim has been to describe something of Soviet architecture's current concerns and of its particularity. Its aspiration to unite society's spiritual interests with its social demands has never been stronger, but that aspiration has to operate through the economic possibilities which prevail nationally and locally. It also operates in the context of a multinational culture. Hence the problem of cultural continuity and consistency within architectural development requires unusual attention, both to its proper content, and to the means of achieving it.

The Soviet Union is a country of unique diversity. It occupies one sixth of the earth's land surface, and the main part of the Eurasian continent. It includes the extremes of Siberia and the subtropics, the Urals, the Far East, Central Asia; it contains forest, steppes, deserts, mountains, vast rivers and lakes. The multitude of nationalities within it have the most diverse ethnocultural characteristics, and an enormously rich legacy of traditions and cultural interactions.

Architecture and town planning have always played an extremely important role in the process of socio-cultural consolidation which brings some unity to the fabric of this country. Our principal tool in achieving this is a social brief. Socially defined norms of architecture and building are the guarantee of democratism, of equality of environmental rights and standards. Thus the most important responsibility which the State has taken on here, and which its latest plans aspire to achieve by the year 2000, is the provision of good-quality housing for all of its citizens.

Construction on a mass scale is the direct result of this, but it poses the architect with a problem of finding an architectural expression for the democratic process, of finding some symbolic interpretation of the social content. This is a tall order. It involves developing a language which will permit architecture to fulfil a dual role: to express the general and the totality, as well as the regional and human specifics. The Soviet profession is not alone amongst the world's architects in being criticised for the modesty of its achievements in this regard, and as papers here show, it is very ready to acknowledge the validity of criticisms, though far from accepting sole responsibility.

If the basic principles of architecture are to answer the main values of society, cultural continuity must be fundamental. What is contributed by today's own practical activity must find some synthesis with what is given us by our traditions, by our heritage. In the 1920s, when Soviet architecture encountered a revolutionary social brief, it considered the problem of establishing a new socialist mode of life to be the decisive and overriding element of its brief. The life-building function of architecture became the key variable in determining how appropriate architectural forms should be generated. At the same time, it acquired a certain stylistic brutality, as it tried to be maximally expressive of the aesthetic possibilities of Functionalism and Constructivism.

Architects of these persuasions rejected the historical heritage on principle, and more perhaps than at any other time in history, architecture set itself up to provoke contrast with its environment. Even then, however, there were individual projects and individual architects who considered symbolic meanings pre-eminent, and addressed themselves to the live sources of tradition and the best examples of architecture which we inherited. One oustanding product of this sensibility was Alexei Shchusev's mausoleum for Lenin on Red Square, which by its form and colour enters into the aesthetic imagery of our capital city and the space of its central square with a subtlety that makes it seem to have grown organically there.

In the space available we can only place this topic on the agenda, and indicate something of what we see to be its subject matter. Some comment is perhaps appropriate, however, about the character of the examples themselves.

With us it has always been the public and community buildings that become the first bearers of the architectural language, fulfilling its spatial, formal and environmental concepts. Thus for Soviet architecture the marker points of the urban environment are the cultural foci: shopping centres, cultural centres, theatres, stadia, department stores − major activity points which spread their aesthetic and functional influence across the whole city or their own district. These objects have a dual life: they belong to the historical environment, to what already exists, and to the contemporary, which is being created now. Thus their architectural significance extends far beyond the framework of any particular interpretation of their direct function, and attempts to address a social requirement at a far deeper level. Where the history of architecture in capitalist societies is very largely a history of private houses, our concern is reflected in a focus upon changing typologies in these public dimensions of the environment. Some of the key variables here are identified in the visual and verbal essays that follow, which look at the changing past of the typologies in pursuit of the deeper cultural continuities which remain valid.

Dr Alexander Kudriavtsev is a Senior Member of the Council of the Union of Architects of the USSR. Dr Alexander Krivov is Deputy Director of the Design Institute of Architecture, Leningrad

CHURCH OF THE SHROUD ON THE RIVER NERL, 12TH CENTURY

Russia adopted Christianity 999 years ago and by that decision entered the orbit of European culture. At that period the many republics of today's Soviet Union were entirely separate nations, and their histories followed very different courses. Thus the development of urban civilisations in Armenia and Georgia started significantly earlier, in the 4th century. The territories of today's Uzbekistan, Tadzhikistan, Turkmenia lay within the sphere of Greek civilisation but their oldest cities are of hardly less antiquity than the Mesopotamian centre of Ur. Southern Siberia and the Altai, like the various cultural groups of the Great Steppe, were in close contact with ancient Chinese civilisation. All these cultural influences interacted with each other, becoming intermingled as they followed the logic of technological and trading developments and the pressures of social factors, submitting to various climatic transformations over the historical period. In the North of Russia proper, in the Black Sea and Caspian steppelands, or in the mountains of the Caucasus alike, the one stable factor was and remains, the landscape, the shape of the terrain.

This constancy of the landscape, amidst all the relatively superficial influences of the human race upon its surroundings, is the source of constancy in architectural traditions in each of the peoples now forming the Soviet Union. Their architectures were open to borrowing from outside, but in borrowing they always preserved a certain internal stability, reworking what was borrowed till it became their own flesh.

If we exclude the oases of Central Asia and the mountain valleys of the Caucasus, the main characteristic of the landscape across the whole Soviet territory was and remains its spaciousness and measurelessness. For this reason one of the main characteristics of Russian architecture has always been the desire to create systems of orientation, visible across considerable distances, which superimposed upon the landscape a human ordering.

The general nature of orientational features is universal, but the impact of scalar differences is significant. It is evident from basic visual psychology that when the average distance between rural hamlets in Russia was 10 to 12 kilometres, and between neighbouring towns 100 kilometres or more, Russian architecture will have developed differently from that in the majority of Western European areas, where analogous spatial dimensions were considerably smaller. More than elsewhere therefore, it

KARELIA *(LEFT)*; SHATILI VILLAGE, KHEVSURETIA, GEORGIA *(RIGHT)*

SELIGER LAKE, NILOVA *(LEFT)*; BALTIC REGION *(RIGHT)*

remained the basic task of the architect, as such a person emerged in the culture, to create the nodes of such an orientational system in the open landscape: it was a function of buildings to show and measure paths across the uninhabited space, to define the extent of human conquest, to help transform the landscape into a man-made artefact. Over the long centuries of conquering the vast territories of this continent our predecessors developed remarkable skill in utilising all the properties of the natural landscape not just for utilitarian ends, but in the pursuit of a harmony, as part of their study of their own place in the world.

We can observe an analogous process in relation to the urban landscape. The more an established town was stretched horizontally by expansion with one- and two-storeyed developments, drawing apart its defensive walls and bastions as they went, the greater became the relative importance of existing tall elements, however small their height in absolute terms. The bold and regular spacing of towers around the town's fortifications contrasted with the extreme fantasy and intricate picturesqueness of the churches and belltowers which rose above the line of the roofs within the town itself, and above the town walls as seen from outside. The natural tendency for towns to gravitate towards defensive sites on high river banks made them visible as a silhouette at distances from one to three kilometres, and their fragmented details progressively enriched the impression with each metre the viewer came closer.

Today mass industrialised housing has come into obvious conflict with this great tradition. When the long reign of 9-, 12- and 16-storeyed housing blocks has destroyed the traditional unity of profile in urban and rural settlements alike, Soviet architects see it as their task to force the construction industry to be flexible and adaptable enough to make possible a restoration of our largely lost skills in the aesthetic handling of natural and urban landscapes. The movement towards recreating these valuable aesthetic traditions is now manifest across the whole country: from the White Sea in the north to the Caspian in the South, from the Carpathian foothills in Western Soviet Union to the Kamchatka peninsula in the Far East, this promises to be one of the strongest influences on our future developments.

PEASANT'S HOUSE, YAKOVLEV, KARELIA, 19TH CENTURY

When the Soviet Union contains about a hundred different nations and nationalities, it may seem at first sight that the labyrinth of paths along which the architecture of its villages has developed must defy analysis. In reality, however, we are dealing with certain large cultural areas, inside which common local characteristics of climate, available materials and resulting activity types amongst the productive population, are of greater significance than characteristics attributable purely to nationality.

In the main tranch we are dealing with the circle of Slavic cultures which have embraced territory right across to the Pacific, including the Baltic group which was historically more closely connected than others to Western Europe, and the Caucasian, created by dozens of small mountain peoples. Elsewhere we have the tranch identified with Central Asian oasis agriculture, that comprising northern nomads and marine hunters, and another of animal husbanders in the steppes. Each of these cultures has its own history, onto which was overlaid in the 1960s a wave of industrially based rural modernisation and the universalised way of life associated with it.

With the exception of the extreme western, European, part of northern Russia from Vologda to Archangel, where there was never any feudal landownership, the rural dwelling of the Slav always remained close to the standard solutions of the logbuilt wooden hut, or *izba*. The spatial and constructional framework of the dwelling did not change significantly according to the inhabitant's economic status. Differences between the poorest and the most affluent in the population were reflected only in the amount of carved decoration applied to the basic structure. Since very early times it had been normal for the peasant's house to be created by professional teams of carpenters on one of a series of standardised models, purchased and transported to the site in demounted form.

First attempts at formulating some idea of a 'model' village date from the 18th century: these aimed to imitate the 'hamlet' in the park at Versailles. Such aspirations to imitate were, however, soon left behind and the typical village plan and form with the church as the dominant element was reproduced unaltered from one generation to the next as it had been before.

In the end of the 18th century and the first three-quarters of the 19th, the life of the privileged classes in Russia was clearly divided into two parts. In winter they lived in the city, in summer on country estates. The city was primarily a place for contact

SAIMONOVO, NR ARCHANGEL, EARLY 1920s *(LEFT)*; S KALINKA, SUDEIKIAI, LITHUANIA, 1981 *(RIGHT)*

V DAVITIA ET AL, KHOKHMATI, GEORGIA, 1982 *(LEFT)*; P IANES, HOUSING AT MERIVIALI, ESTONIA, 1974 *(RIGHT)*

with the achievements of culture. The country estate was a place for communicating with neighbours and for one's own intensive creative activity. Russian poetry, drama, literature were born of the country estate, and at the end of the 19th century, increasingly of the surburban *dacha*. At the present time the country estates are very appropriately used as places of collective leisure, which often includes, for the professional and artistic groups, precisely such concentrated creative work as they saw previously.

There have been attempts to improve the planning of villages ever since the Revolution and particularly in the 1930s and 1940s, but as a result of the extreme inadequacies of resources the concepts have never got much further than paper – and the film-sets of Sergei Eisenstein. Nonetheless, it provided valuable experience which has been available as a resource during the last few years, when there has been a return to tackling the practicalities of total reconstruction of the rural settlements. Alongside the investigations of possible housing and service structures, a constantly recurrent theme of architectural exploration has been the question of the village's social centre. In the absence of multi-storeyed dwellings, even social centres in buildings of small physical dimensions acquire great significance in the architecture of such small settlements.

The absurd tendency of the 1960s to erect multi-storeyed housing in rural areas was happily discarded very rapidly. It is interesting to see how now, when various types of single-family house are being introduced, the practice of individualising the houses with external decoration is emerging again with new vigour.

Urbanisation across the whole country has already reached a level where the appeal of nature for the city-dweller produces a regular town-country migration on his days off and during summer holidays. A gigantic network of sanatoria, national parks, camping sites and tourist centres, all created in various ways by the state, has covered virtually the whole country, turning it into what one might call an extended service zone. This has created a new field of design activity for the architect, as well as the planning requirement to develop the whole settlement network across the continent in an integrated way. Today the question of rural architecture cannot be tackled, either functionally or aesthetically, in isolation from the problems arising in other fields of architectural activity.

I ANUSHKIAVICHUS, ZHIOGIALIS HOLIDAY CENTRE, LITHUANIA, 1974-8

FROM LEFT TO RIGHT: PEASANT HOUSE, OSHENEVO, KARELIA, 1876; A ALVER, LOKS HOLIDAY CENTRE, ESTONIA, 1981; MUSEUM OF VILLAGE LIFE, LITHUANIA

D ZHILIARDI, R KAZAKOV, KUZMINKI COUNTRY ESTATE NR MOSCOW, 1820-45

CARVED WINDOW, GONCHAROVA, MOSCOW, IN 1920S

D ZHILIARDI, GARDEN PAVILION, MOSCOW, 1829-31

K BLANK, BALLROOM, KUSKOVO, NR MOSCOW, 1751-77

A MIKHAILOV, O BOVE, BOLSHOI THEATRE, MOSCOW, 1821-4

The art of theatre became established in Russia long before it had any special buildings. Dramatised bible stories were acted out in Russian churches from the late 15th century, but secular theatre, facing stiff opposition from the Orthodox church, only took hold in Russia somewhat later. The first strolling artistes would perform wherever people were prepared to stop and watch, against the natural sets of the landscape or architecture around them. By the 18th century temporarily erected, demountable booths were used to stage small productions for the simple townfolk at times of fairs and religious festivals. The first timber building erected for theatre in Russia was that erected on Red Square in 1702, during Peter the Great's reign.

Thereafter, the Imperial theatres and dozens of theatrical auditoria created in palaces and country mansions supplied the needs of the nobility. Democratisation of the theatre led to the construction of public auditoria with the familiar tripartite structure of stalls, balcony and gallery which we see in notable examples such as the Sheremetev family's Ostankino Palace in Moscow, the Yusupov Palace in Petersburg, as well as the first provincial public theatre in Yaroslavl. In the majority of urban theatres, the buildings were treated as the centrepiece, the

excuse, for a major formal ensemble, and the centrality of their cultural role was expressed by making them the focus of a whole system of streets and public spaces.

The 19th century continued this partiality for the theatre, treating it as something spiritually exalted, as a genuine 'temple of the arts'. By the beginning of the 20th century, however, Russian theatre was beginning to develop in new directions. After the 1917 Revolution the development of theatre received a new impulse: the companies formed around such directors as Meyerkhold, Tairov and Vakhtangov reflected the desire of innovative directors for a greater diversity of scenic possibilities and with that, for different organisations of the theatrical space. There were experiments with theatricalised mass 'events' in various towns all over the county, while in Moscow, Kharkov and Novosibirsk in particular there were experiments in whole new kinds of theatre building. National theatres were consciously established with new buildings in virtually all the Soviet republics. All this led even to a certain over-exaggeration not only of the theatre's symbolic role, but of the role of theatre buildings in architecture and town planning. A classic example of this is the Red Army Theatre in Moscow, designed by

53

A MIKHAILOV, O BOVE, BOLSHOI THEATRE: AUDITORIUM

Alabian and Simbirtsev in 1934, whose plan is the shape of a five-pointed star. Needless to say it required enormous inventiveness and some tough compromises to insert the complex organism of a theatre into the sharp-angled, tight spaces of this so-symbolic predetermined plan form.

Today we are seeing the growth of new little studio theatres, functioning in the basements of high-rise housing blocks as the focus of club activities, similar to the post-Revolutionary auditoria created within workers' clubs. These provide an alternative to the individualised theatre space, still preserved with the larger, more formal, companies. This is the tradition which gave birth to the new building of the Moscow Arts Theatre, MKhAT, whose stylistic treatment acknowledges the traditions of Russian Art Nouveau, or Moderne, and thereby refers us back to MKhAT's original building for Stanislavsky. The same tradition underlies the conception of the recently reconstructed Taganka Theatre in Moscow, which has successfully solved the problem of a transformable action space for the theatre of the 1980s. In a similar category are the highly expressive, purpose-built premises of Obraztsov's world-famous puppet theatre, of Lurov's wild animal theatre, of Natalia Sats' Children's Musical Theatre, or

the theatre in Viliandi – just a few amongst the many new theatre buildings in the Soviet Union.

In recent decades the town planning aspects of theatre building have been considerably enriched again, but given a new and wider interpretation. Where the traditional concept insisted that a whole new 'theatre square' had to be an integral part of the project for any new theatre, we have now established as a legitimate concept the more active notion of a 'theatricalised urban environment'. Young Soviet architects and students have used the opportunity of international design competitions to formulate the ideas that the theatrical ensemble of the future should be an unprecedented type of 'theatrical town'. The concept proposes a linking together of the stages of the traditional theatres by new playing spaces, so that the real town as it were becomes absorbed into the midst of a mass theatrical activity.

Common to all these projects is the pursuit of new ways to distribute viewing points and performance sites so as to establish direct contact between actors and audience. The humanistic and populist principles in these projects suggests that these are trends which will prevail in the theatres of tomorrow.

K ALABIAN, V SIMBIRTSEV, RED ARMY THEATRE, MOSCOW, 1934-40

A ANISIMOV, IU GNEDOVSKY, TAGANKA THEATRE, MOSCOW, 1979

A NEKRASOV, A CHELTSOV ET AL, RECONSTRUCTION OF MAYAKOVSKY THEATRE, 1986

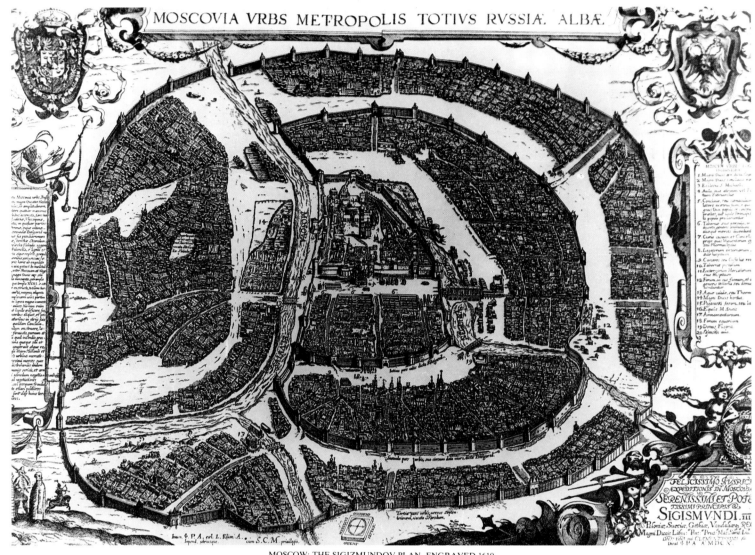

MOSCOW: THE SIGIZMUNDOV PLAN, ENGRAVED 1610

The compact, high-density towns of the mountain valleys are an extreme minority amongst the settlement types occurring in the Soviet Union, where most human settlements have always been located in the plains, with the housing areas frequently separated by water meadows and gardens. For centuries, therefore, the most distinctive characteristic of Russian urbanism was its stretched-out, thin-spread quality.

Thanks to the way it merged urban forms into nature, Russian medieval town planning could sometimes more accurately be called landscape planning. Right up to the end of the 19th century urban form was characterised by the dominance of low-rise building spread thinly amidst the greenery and following the relief of the terrain. Equally important, it was integrally linked with the surrounding natural environment by the fact that untreated, largely unshaped timber formed the physical mass of the vast majority of its buildings. Amidst the matrix of these timber structures the little parish churches, freestanding with their high belfries, created a contrasting rhythm that was picked up and enlarged by the towers of fortress walls and the larger multi-domed stone churches and belltowers. The Russian town was a form scattered across the plain or spread along the banks

of a deep, peacefully flowing river whose horizontals were repeated by those of monastery walls.

Since earliest times the settlements in northern Russia, where natural conditions are extreme, had been distinguished by a closer clustering in their silhouette. This feature was characteristic of the new Siberian settlements that arose at the turn of the 17th and 18th centuries, rapidly built on regular street plans by government land-surveyors using standard planning 'templates'.

St Petersburg was founded in 1702 as a new, European-style city, consciously contrasted to the traditional Russian type. Here the components were 'model' developments with uniform cornice lines, straight streets, solidly developed plots, and the chilly stiffness of the whole scene contrasted markedly with the open looseness of the traditional urban landscape. During the next hundred years over 400 regularly planned towns were established and realised using these principles in miniature. In their form they splendidly reflected the union of tradition with innovation: the picturesque silhouettes of the traditional Russian town were created on the basis of a regular plan.

The development of industry from the end of the 17th century to the middle of the 19th took place primarily ouside Russia's

THE MEDIEVAL TOWN OF GOROKHOVETS FROM THE NEARBY HILLS

towns and cities, on virgin sites with special industrial villages. When the industrial boom began in the cities in the 1880s, the traditional 'scatteredness' was not just preserved; it was very frequently reinforced still further.

The First World War, the 1917 Revolution, the Civil War, the Second World War all caused significant changes to the urban landscape. The war of 1941-45 left behind ruins. The years following it were a time for the passionate restoration of elements of value in the urban landscape, for establishing new urban priorities. The medieval Russian towns of Novgorod and Pskov rose again out of ruined piles. The razed cities of Volgograd, Minsk, Kiev were effectively created afresh from nothing.

In the 1950s there were attempts to recreate the traditional urban silhouettes on much vaster, 'modern' scales. The so-called High Buildings of Moscow, with their spires rising to the clouds, became the new visual dominants of the city. The urban profile of the capital started to include such picturesque elements as the great radial boulevards or 'prospects', vast new green areas of parkland and the newly secured and developed river embankments.

In the 1960s, when the sphere of influence of architects was

notably narrowed, and when the 'engineering period' of standardised town planning solutions began, there was a new strengthening of the historical tendency towards thinness of spread in urban development. However there started to be increasing concern about the fate of the urban space as an aesthetic dimension of the whole organism: about the fate of its whole hierachy of values; its structure as an object in the landscape; its rhythms and colour schemes.

In the new towns of Siberia and the Volga area such as Brezhnev, Togliatti and Shevchenko, all of which were certainly founded on progressive principles in their day, the shortcomings of inadequate flexibility in the spatial solutions have started to become all too evident. So too has the hypertrophied scale of the housing areas, the lack of low-rise building which has created such monotony of the urban silhouette. At the present time Soviet architects are ever more actively juxtaposing to this density and fixity the traditional merits of thin development. They are speaking out increasingly sharply against these forms in the language of economics, and protesting against the cultural stereotype which sees the urban space as no more than a dense environment for mere existence.

FROM TOP TO BOTTOM: PANORAMIC VIEW OF THE SERGIEV SETTLEMENT (*POSAD*) NEAR ZAGORSK; PANOF

OF ST PETERSBURG, FROM ENGRAVING OF MAKHAEV, MID 18TH CENTURY PANORAMIC VIEW OF MOSCOW, 1980s

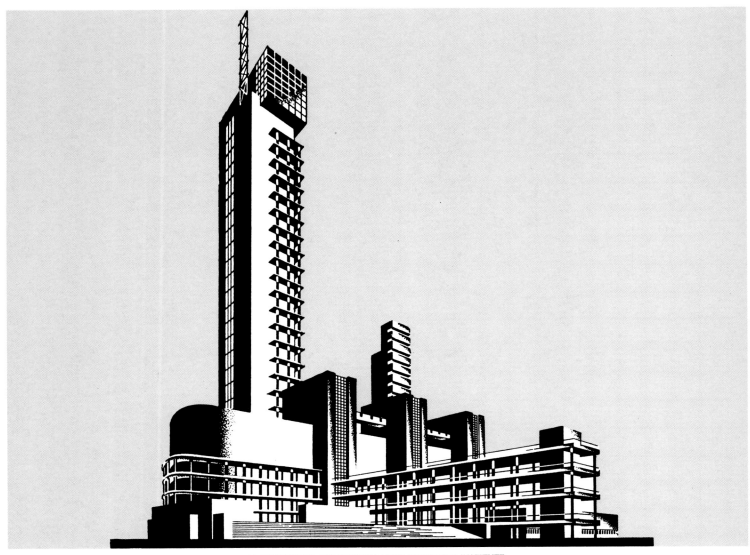

IA CHERNIKOV: PROJECT FOR A STATE HYGIENE INSTITUTE

'He who has never been to the top of Ivan the Great's tower, and never had the opportunity to survey the entirety of our ancient capital from end to end at one glance; he who has never once feasted his eyes upon this majestic, almost boundless panorama, can have no understanding of what Moscow is. Moscow is not a silent mass of stones assembled, coldly, in symmetrical patterns. No! She has a unique spirit entirely her own, her own life. Every stone of her preserves an inscription, written in it by time and fate, an inscription incomprehensible to the madding crowd but rich, fecund with ideas, with feelings, with inspiration for the scholar, the patriot and the poet!' Thus wrote the Russian poet Lermontov in his youth, in 1833, after climbing the 80 metres of Moscow's main vertical structure – the belltower of Ivan the Great in the Kremlin. His lines suffuse life into the analytic notion of the monocentric structure typical of the Russian town, of which Moscow is the classic example.

Moscow's urban development was carried out on the basis of a radial plan centred on this tower, with streets running outwards from it, defined by the Kremlin's own towers, and beyond them, the triumphal arches and other ceremonial gates to the city. Beyond this, the radial form was further reinforced by the ring

of defensive monasteries, each marked by its own high belltower.

The new era marked by the town planning innovations of Peter the Great supplemented this theme with other devices. The pointed spires of his Admiralty and the Peter and Paul church, like masts on one of Peter's ships in the Neva estuary, fixed the most important foci in the plan of this new northern capital based on Western European models. The capacity of these needle-like verticals to organise movement along a street can be traced back to the devices of medieval Russian town planning, but more important was the way in which they augmented and emphasised the key nodes and intersection points in the city's multi-focal street pattern.

Another high-point in the subjugation of the historical city was the introduction of the Baroque belltowers by Rastrelli and Ukhtomsky. Their powerful and magnificent upward movement – although never taken as far as intended because the 140 metre-high belltower for the Smolny was never built – make them one of the most potent achievements of Russian architecture. By the first half of the 19th century this kind of slender vertical, which had become one of the most important elements

BELLTOWER, NOVODEVICHY CONVENT, MOSCOW, 1690s   V TATLIN, MONUMENT TO THE 3RD INTERNATIONAL, 1919   V KRINSKY, VSNKh SKYSCRAPER, 1922-3

of the urban composition, was supplemented by large high volumes of buildings which themselves aspired to the role of visual dominants. St Isaac's Cathedral in St Petersburg by Montferrand was one such example, and the Cathedral of Christ the Saviour in Moscow by Ton was another. Their scalar relationship to the general fabric of the city was of the same nature as that created in the mid 16th century by the erection of St Basil's cathedral on Moscow's Red Square.

In this century it was the essence of Tatlin's Monument to the Third International, conceived in 1919, that it represented an affirmation of the revolutionary victories and of new aesthetic principles by a similar formal gesture. The naked boldness of the conception, the unprecedented height and manner of construction, so dissimilar to the vast skyscrapers of Manhattan from that date, make this tower a truly remarkable scheme – a genuine Tower of Babylon for the 20th century. The so-called 'Soviet Skyscrapers' that appeared in the projects of students from the Vkhutemas and Vkhutein, the futuristic ideas of Malevich, Chernikhov, Krinsky, the forward-looking visions of Leonidov and Melnikov, were to be only the beginning of the long list of names and buildings which would develop the idea of the vertical during the 1920s and 1930s.

The War of 1941-45 prevented the real incarnation of this theme intended in the vast volume of the Palace of Soviets project alongside the Kremlin in Moscow. This 210 metre-high Palace, conceived as a grandiose pedestal to a 100 metre statue of Lenin, was to create a new focal centre for the capital on analogy with the Ivan belltower of the medieval city and just upstream of it. Later this historical analogy came to be embodied in the ring of seven High Buildings constructed in the 1950s, which very precisely reproduced the traditional system of visual landmarks of the old Russian town, and a similar enhancement of the city's radial-concentric plan structure.

In recent decades the pursuit of an expressive and meaningful form for the dominant vertical elements of the urban silhouette has not produced satisfactory results. By ceasing to treat them individually, in respect of both design and location, and by throwing away their function as main buildings determining the identity and image of specific places, as well as by raising the overall height of urban development, our town planners have totally undermined their status as special elements of the city with a distinctive and important spatial function.

A BRODSKY, I UTKIN, 'GLASS TOWER' COMPETITION PROJECT, 2ND PRIZE, 1985

A SILCHENKO, STUDY IN DYNAMISM, 1924

KREMLIN, MOSCOW, FROM GREAT STONE BRIDGE, MID 19TH CENTURY

D CHECHULIN, HOUSING COMPLEX, MOSCOW, 1952

A DUSHKIN ET AL, GOVERNMENT OFFICES, MOSCOW, 1951

I LEONIDOV, COMPETITION PROJECT FOR HEAVY INDUSTRY COMMISSARIAT, 1934

M POSOKHIN ET AL, COMECON BUILDING, MOSCOW, 1963-70

KREMLIN, MOSCOW, LATE 19TH CENTURY

NEVSKY PROSPECT, ST PETERSBURG, WITH ANICHKOV PALACE: LITHOGRAPH BY BESAMEN, MID-19TH CENTURY

City streets have been compared to almost everything. They are rivers, flowing out into the estuaries of squares; they are blood vessels penetrating the living organism which is the city. To some people they are merely transport routes, to others places for leisurely pottering from one shop window to the next or even a kind of open-air club for meeting and chatting with friends. In these respects the Soviet street is hardly unique today. Historically, however, the situation in Russia itself was very different. There, the traditional street was for centuries a narrow route with rough timber surfacing that ran between continuous wooden fences, devoid of social functions. The monotony of the fencing was broken by entrance gates, and decorative wooden carvings, and the sombre background of dark timber was relieved by the belltowers, spires and golden domes of churches, and the white stone mansions of urban notables.

The construction of St Petersburg introduced to Russia the European type of street, more or less continuously developed on both sides with masonry building. That city's main street, Nevsky Prospect, formed one of the rays of a giant trident in the ground plan of the city, focused on the golden spire of the Admiralty at the point where the Neva's water merges with the Baltic.

The Nevsky Prospect was perceived, for all its straightness, not as a transport artery but as a favourite place of promenading and festive processions. That is probably why the old engravings depict it constantly swinging back and forth in an endless ribbon, proudly displaying its architecture and populated in the foreground by carriages and promenading couples.

The traditions of the Nevsky Prospect were reborn in the 1950s when the building of new towns and the reconstruction of war-damaged cities was taking place all over the country, and monumental colonnades and porticos, luxuriant spires and towers proliferated. The immense width of the great new 'prospects' was destined not for the leisure of pedestrians but for rushing motorcars, parades and processions.

Time passed, however, and the themes of classical architecture were banished from the drawing board. The influence of Le Corbusier led to a situation where rectangular prisms, 'with all sides bathed in light and fresh air', started to multiply even faster as they became increasingly indistinguishable from each other.

A particular landmark was the creation of Kalinin Prospect in Central Moscow – in its way an imaginative compromise be-

A GUTNOV, Z KHARITONOVA ET AL, RENOVATION AND PEDESTRIANISATION OF ARBAT ST, MOSCOW, 1984-5

tween the traditional street of facades and the ideas of freestanding towers rising amidst the green. But the new Prospect sliced through the old fabric unceremoniously and, having followed the example of Haussmann in Paris, its authors received the same reproofs and reproaches. The reconstruction of the historic fabric currently underway in a great many Soviet towns, is seen by architects as an alternative approach to the ideas embodied in the Kalinin Prospect, in line with the preservation of the old city and the creation of maximum convenience and pleasure for pedestrians. Recent examples of this approach are the reconstruction of Arbat Street, which runs parallel to Kalinin Prospect in downtown Moscow, and of the old districts of central Tbilisi in Georgia.

With the advance of technology some of the street's traditional functions have been taken over by the underground metro systems in bigger cities. The General Plan for the Reconstruction of Moscow, which was developed from 1931 onwards, included the creation of a metro system amongst first-priority tasks for the city, and in 1935 construction of the first line started with a series of stations at very great depth. Today the Moscow metro system has some two hundred stations over a large sub-regional area.

The metro always meant more than a mere solution to transportation problems. It was seen as a symbol of the radical modernisation of a previously backward country. Its stations, whose design involved the very best architects, were treated as models for buildings of the future, contrasting sharply in their splendour with the still very poor conditions of everyday life. This conception thrived right up to the late 1950s, when the temporary celebration of the functionalist doctrines brought the death of such a vision. The next new stations were nothing but transportation nodes.

As the populations of other cities have grown, new metro systems have been created in the diverse climates and cultures of Leningrad, Kiev, Tbilisi, Kharkov, Erevan, Baku, Minsk, Tashkent and Novosibirsk. This process has coincided with the rejection of narrow functionalism in architecture, and in these new systems, albeit in more restrained forms than before, we have seen the traditions of the first Moscow lines reborn. Each station is treated as a public building of high aesthetic significance, and the cities take care to secure the resources for giving high levels of artistic individuality to their metro systems.

L POLIAKOV, ARBATSKAIA METRO STATION, MOSCOW, 1952

N LADOVSKY, RED GATES METRO STATION, MOSCOW, 1935

A SHCHUSEV, KOMSOMOLSKAIA METRO STATION, MOSCOW, 1946-52

V GELFREIKH, I ROZHIN, ELEKTROZAVODSKAIA METRO, MOSCOW, 1944

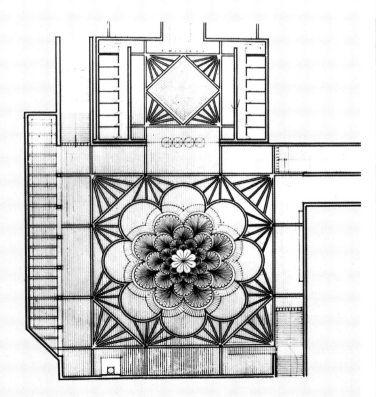

D TOROSIAN, M MIASIAN, VESTIBULE OF LENIN SQUARE METRO, EREVAN, 1981

M POSOKHIN, A MNDOIANTS ET AL, KALININ PROSPECT, MOSCOW, 1962-8

G BATIASHVILI, SH KAVLASHVILI ET AL, RECONSTRUCTION OF OLD TBILISI, 1980

G BARAVIKAS, N KOVAVSKENE, MOSCOW CINEMA, VILNIUS, 1975

HOUSING ON GORKY STREET, VILNIUS, LITHUANIA

RECONSTRUCTION OF THE OLD CITY, TALLIN, ESTONIA

THE SQUARE

CATHEDRAL SQUARE IN THE KREMLIN, MOSCOW

Squares are the main public spaces of a town. They are its interiors, reception rooms accessible to all. Their architectural organisation is more difficult than that of any individual building. Unlike the street, the square is a concrete place, a specific experience in its own right with its own distinctive image. For that reason it has always been more prestigious to live in one of the buildings surrounding a square than to live on a street.

Trading squares throughout the world are much the same, but squares that are public spaces are quite different. Each has a distinctive cultural function as well as its own particular architectural interpretation of that role. Over the course of centuries the strong subordination of urban affairs directly to centralised bureaucracies meant that Russia never developed the building type so characteristic of Western European towns – the Town Hall. In Russian the function of such a building as proclamation point was fulfilled at first by the covered external galleries and stairs (called *kryltso*) of the local nobleman's palace. Later, special structures called *lobnye mesta*, literally places of execution, would be erected, whence decrees and enactments of the government could be read to the public.

For many centuries the site for the most important and celebratory state event in Russia as a whole was the cathedral square in Moscow's Kremlin. Even after the capital was transferred to St Petersburg all coronations of Russian tsars took place here in Russia's architecturally most 'special' public space. The surrounding cathedrals themselves gave the ceremony an important element of its sacredness, and their tiered, upward moving composition with complete absence of horizontal cornices wiped out any visual barrier between earth and sky.

The building of St Petersburg took place in the Baroque and classicist periods, and led to the creation there of a space for the sanctifying of power, in the form of Palace Square behind the Winter Palace, which was regular and symmetrical in form. To a greater or lesser extent, Palace Square thereafter found a structural imitation in every district administrative centre in the country.

The historical models of the public square were examined afresh in the period of post-Revolutionary reconstruction. Perhaps the first important, though modest, example of an innovative approach was the reconstruction of Soviet Square, in front of the city hall, in Shchusev's New Moscow plan of 1923. In part it was realised, but unfortunately the square is not pre-

KARL ROSSI, PALACE SQUARE, LENINGRAD, 1818-29

served in its original form since the ceremonial propylaea were demolished, and the obelisk in honour of the first Soviet Constitution was replaced by an equestrian statue of Moscow's original founder, Prince Iuri Dolgoruky.

The Soviet Square project was classical in spirit, but soon the romantic story of Constructivism attracted even such seemingly steadfast pillars of academicism as Shchusev and his contemporary Zholtovsky. Fascinated by the possibilities of functional volumetric combinations and by devising whole new types of towns, the Constructivists paid little attention to anything so traditional as the city square. Nonetheless there is one example of a purely Modernist, Constructivist urban space of this kind, in Dzerzhinsky Square in Kharkov. Sergei Einstein used its adjoining Gosprom building as stage-set for his film *The General Line*, to create the image of the new socialist Moscow.

After the Second World War the design of squares became one of the most prestigious aspects of architectural practice. In the conditions of post-War ruination it was impossible to provide everyone with housing, but in return, as it were, what was immediately created for the inhabitants of the cities were the central streets, squares, theares, clubs, metro stations – all

designed with maximum possible effort and attention. In Minsk and Vologda squares were created in front of single major buildings. In the newly rebuilt towns of Alma-Ata, of Frunze or Ashkhabad, the new squares were closely integrated with whole complexes of public buildings. More recently, for example in Yaroslavl, architects have been noticeably seeking to link new building spatially and stylistically with the irregular compositions of the historic fabric of the inherited squares.

After the 1917 Revolution, Red Square took on itself the function of principal forum for the nation's state events. Its ancient name Krasnaya Square, meaning Beautiful Square, has the alternative meaning of Red Square, which prophetically coincided with the colour signifying the politics of the new state, and the colour of its banners. In softer form it is also the colour of the Kremlin's brick wall which forms the longest side of the space. Once a trading square, Red Square thus became, and remains, the focal point and destination of celebratory processions and state events in the Soviet capital, as well as a necropolis for the country's leaders and most prominent citizens. In this extreme 'specialness', it is an archetype for the central forum of every lesser city and town in the Soviet Union.

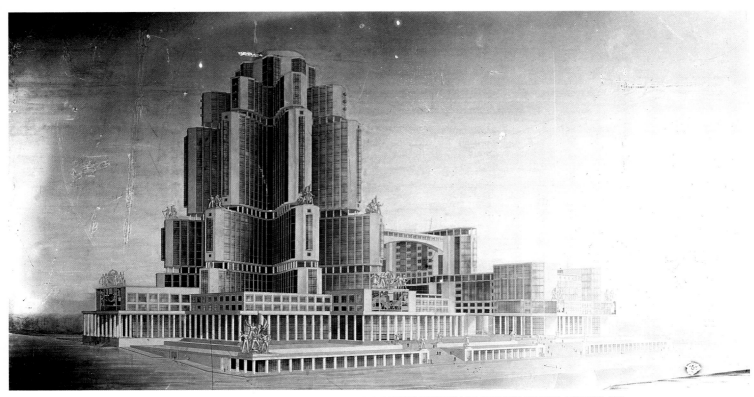

V & A VESNIN, 2ND COMPETITION PROJECT FOR HEAVY INDUSTRY COMMISSARIAT ON RED SQUARE, MOSCOW, 1934

V & A VESNIN, 1ST COMPETITION PROJECT FOR HEAVY INDUSTRY COMMISSARIAT ON RED SQUARE, MOSCOW, 1934

I FOMIN, M MINKUS, PROJECT FOR KOLKHOZ SQUARE AROUND THE SUKHAREV TOWER: ENTRANCE FROM THE SOUTH

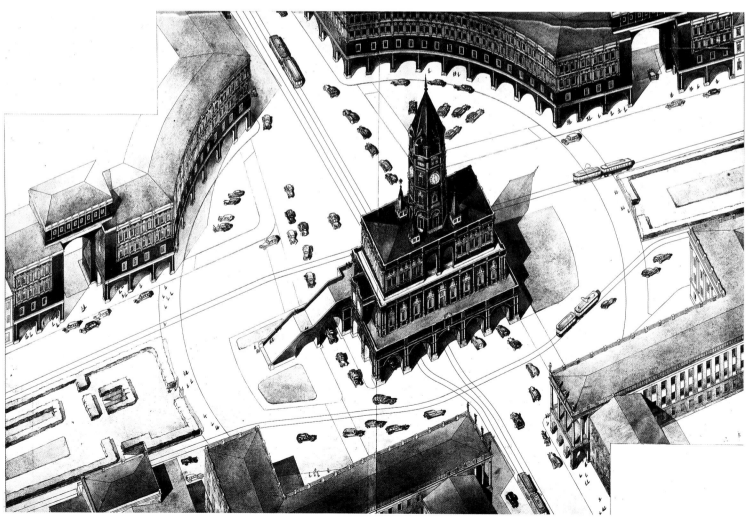

I FOMIN, M MINKUS, PROJECT FOR KOLKHOZ SQUARE AROUND THE SUKHAREV TOWER: AERIAL VIEW

SMOLENSK SQUARE, MOSCOW, WITH BRIDGE OVER MOSCOW RIVER, AND HIGH BUILDING OF EARLY 50s

SMOLENSK SQUARE, MOSCOW: ORIGINAL PERSPECTIVE AND DETAIL

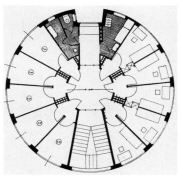

L KEKUSHEV, APARTMENT HOUSE, MOSCOW, 1906; I MALOZEMOV, GREAT ZAPOROZHE, 1930; 'CUPBOARD APARTMENTS' PROJECT, 1929   A MALINOVSKY,   HOUSING, 1910s

The October Revolution of 1917 gave birth to an unprecedented explosion of creative activity, and architecture constituted one of the most fertile fields. A vast diversity of new architectural ideas emerged in this period, ranging from projects for complete flying cities by the Vkhutemas student Krutikov to so-called 'cupboard housing' where the individual's living accommodation was reduced to a mere cell with the minimum area for a bed and a work table, and all toilet and cooking facilities were communal. The age of individual villas was dead, and the last individual house to approach the old space standards was built by the young architect Melnikov, demonstrating the new approaches to organising living space around which 20th-century architecture was revolving elsewhere, in combination with very traditional Russian building methods. But most of the building effort at that date went into innumerable large housing blocks and hostels for the younger workers.

As the process of reconstructing society on socialist lines began, it drew a flood of people into the towns from the countryside, and that process in turn generated a multitude of new ideas in the field of housing design. Architects pursued a wide range of different credos, with the older ones continuing to reproduce their Garden Cities or their Radiant Cities of sky-scrapers, agreeing only in their rejection of the old-style specu-lative apartment block which had come to supplant low-rise housing in Russian town centres under the last decade of capital-ism before the Revolution. Some architects were impelled by a rather simplified understanding of social policies to build 'com-munal houses' of minimal living space and maximum shared facilities. Others, preoccupied with economic realism, focused their attention particularly on devising the cheapest possible ranges of dwelling types through maximum standardisation.

The return to traditional classical styles on the 1940s and 1950s enriched Soviet towns with new housing blocks of richly three-dimensional facades and vigorous overall silhouettes. The use of such decorative elements as the classical Orders and a diversity of finishing materials made housing construction to expensive to be compatible with a solution of the housing problem, whose quantitative dimension had been worsened still further by the destruction wrought in the Second World War. The way out of this situation was found in a changeover to prefabricated building techniques. Five-storeyed housing, far from beautiful, as cheap as possible and with small individual

A VLASOV ET AL, KRESHCHATKA STREET, KIEV, 1949

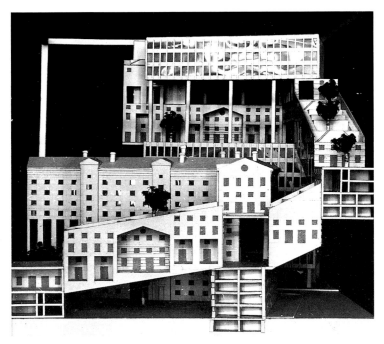

A NEKRASOV ET AL, 'URBAN SPACE OF THE FUTURE', 1980

V CHEKANAUSKAS ET AL, LAZDINAI HOUSING, VILNIUS, 1967-73

INTERIOR OF THE 1950s

apartments, did make it possible to move people out of the earlier communal apartments and the pre-revolutionary basements of the city centres.

Characteristic of the whole Soviet period has been the pursuit of the most rapid possible solution of the housing problem through providing people with virtually free homes with standard amenities. The burdensome legacies of the War held back this process, but did not stop it. The continuous enhancement of various series of standardised units had led to a gradual improvement in the planning of the apartments themselves, which have by now achieved sensible organisations of activity spaces and relatively spacious kitchens and halls. The present housing construction programme envisages that by the year 2000 every Soviet family will at last have been provided with its own separate apartment or individual house.

The main focus of house building in the Soviet Union is currently the old town centres, where the reconstruction of new buildings requires quite new design ideas and technical approaches. This challenge has called forth a wave of particular interest in the conceptual projects of the young architects, who are leading the search for ways of reconstructing these old areas of the city centre.

A typically futuristic project entitled 'New urban space', that was designed for the First World Biennale in Sofia in 1980, set itself the task of reconstructing the city with the help of what is called 'street-buildings'. Around the perimeter of an imaginary cube, picking up storey height as it goes, the 'street-building' rises upwards, hanging in the air, descending below the ground, intersecting with neighbouring structures. A whole series of city functions are transferred into the 'street-building' and some storeys of it are transformed into open terraces and public squares. Thus the familiar spatial scale is restored to a fragment of the city, with the creation of a network of new streets and public spaces.

Now, as we approach the 1990s, the architecture of housing is entering a new phase. The architectural vocabulary of housing construction is constantly expanding: we are again beginning to see housing built of brick, techniques with monolithic concrete are expanding, lifted up storey by storey. At last systems of prefabricated construction are becoming more flexible, and we see the start of a nationalist trend away from high-rise development towards lower forms more akin with tradition.

A ROCHEGOV, M BYLINKIN ET AL, HOUSING OF STANDARD 'BOX' UNITS, VORONTSOVO, MOSCOW, 1980s

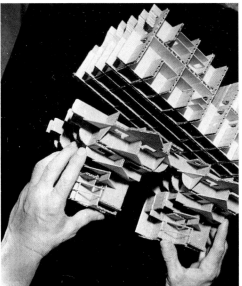

BRICK HOUSING, UDALTSOV STREET, MOSCOW, LATE 1970s   A GNEZDILOV, ADAPTING 5-STOREYED HOUSING, 1986   N ZAKHARINA ET AL, PUSHKIN, NR LENINGRAD, 1984

77

NATIONAL EXHIBITIONS

G LEZHAVA, A KURDIANI, GEORGIAN PAVILION, AGRICULTURAL EXHIBITION, MOSCOW, 1937

V LISITSYN, MEAT & DAIRY PAVILION, AGRICULTURAL EXHIBITION, MOSCOW, 1954

K MELNIKOV, USSR PAVILION, PARIS, 1925

B IOFAN, V MUKHINA, USSR PAVILION, 1937

K MELNIKOV, TOBACCO PAVILION, MOSCOW, 1923

The phenomenon of the industrial exhibition was a product of the industrial revolution of the 18th and 19th centuries, and of the pursuit of markets by the capitalist industry which created it. Their inspiration and prototype lay in the trading fairs whose history stretched well back into the Middle Ages, and the first of the great international exhibitions, in London's Crystal Palace in 1851, left an indelible impression on the numerous Russian visitors. From the beginning , whether national or international, the industrial exhibitions were not just places for demonstrating technical progress. They were simultaneously a new type of cultural festival, and as such a place for cultural self-advertisement. Thus for many years, the style of Russian pavilions at the earliest international exhibitions emphasised the 'nationalistic' features of Russian timber architecture.

At the All-Russian Exhibition in 1896, however, there was a break, and a new direction was established for the future when the famous engineer Shukhov created a highly original spatial structure in metal. This was to be the start of a new tradition whereby these exhibition pavilions were used as a kind of dress-rehearsal or testing-ground for new architectural forms. Very naturally these pavilions came to bear a heavy symbolic

load as a result.

The first All-Russian Exhibition of Agriculture and Handicraft Industries, held in Moscow in 1923, was created on the site of the city's former rubbish dump, which is now Gorky Park. This first such national event of the Soviet era was particularly distinguished architecturally by Melnikov's pavilion of the Far East. For reasons of simplicity and economy quite as much as aesthetics, the majority of pavilions here had their timber structure of columns, beams and girders exposed to the viewer's gaze, creating a strong feeling of 'construction' that echoed very aptly the state of the nation at that date.

At the Paris Exhibition of Decorative Arts in 1925 Melnikov's pavilion for the USSR, whose colours and interior design were by Rodchenko, was the only one apart from Le Corbusier's for *l'Esprit Nouveau*, which made a clear statement of the ideology of Modern architecture. After the end of the exhibition it was given to the French trades union organisation for re-erection in central Paris, where for a long time it did actually serve as a workers' club.

Even more emphatically symbolic was the Soviet pavilion in Paris 12 years later, in the World Fair of 1937, which coincided

V ANDREEV, I TARANOV, MECHANISATION PAVILION, AGRICULTURAL EXHIBITION, MOSCOW, 1954

A TAMANIAN, JUBILEE EXHIBITION, YAROSLAVL, 1913

IU ABRAMOV, A POLIANSKY, USSR PAVILION, BRUSSELS, 1958

with the 20th anniversary of the Revolution. Here the entire building was transformed into a highly original pedestal for the colossal sculptural work by Vera Mukhina depicting an industrial worker and a female collective farmer energetically raising upward the hammer and sickle as symbols of their liberation. The composition expressed their energetic husbanding of the Soviet land as well as the youth of the nation itself and the drama of its relentless drive forward.

When a major exhibition park was laid out in Moscow for the All-Union Agricultural Exhibition of 1939, which demonstrated the achievements of the collective farm programme, the architectural treatment of the numerous republican pavilions reflected the current nationwide celebration of a synthesis between the national and the classical, and the post-war recreation of the exhibition of 1954 brought this process to a culmination. The colourful luxuriance of the vernacular traditions were worked together with the more precise and defined stylisation of classical Greek models. Eclectic references drawn from the whole heritage of the Soviet republics' architecture were enriched and supplemented by the insertion into them of 'agricultural' images. Architectural elements

took on the forms of ears of corn, sheaves of wheat, animal heads and so on, as decorativeness became the main feature of the aesthetic.

From the beginning of the 1960s until now, we have seen in the architecture of exhibitions the shift between two trends: the depictive, symbolic approach, of which the Soviet pavilion at Osaka was an example, and the utilitarian, exemplified by the Brussels pavilion of 1958 and the Montreal building of 1967, where the accent is transferred from the external forms to the content – to the objects demonstrating the country's economic, technological and cultural progress. After the culmination of symbolism in Osaka, the tendency away from the national-romantic treatment of architectural forms in favour of the communicative has recently become increasingly pronounced.

Exhibition architecture always has a temporary character. But this does not prevent it from reflecting the development of its own culture and society with great clarity, precisely because of its concentrated, almost poster-like form. In Soviet architecture these pavilions, both at home and abroad, have always reflected the front line, the innovative trend within Soviet architecture of their period.

I VOZNESENSKY, A BOKOV, CONSUMER GOODS PAVILION, VDNKh EXHIBITION OF ECONOMIC ACHIEVEMENT, MOSCOW, 1986

F SHEKHTEL, RUSSIAN PAVILION, GLASGOW, 1901

L EVZOVICH, M KHAISMAN, RECONSTRUCTING VDNKh: PROJECT, 1980